Berlitz®

Egypt

Front cover: Two of the four seated
colossi of Ramesses II at Abu Simbel

Right: Fresco of Ramesses III in the
Valley of Kings at Thebes

TOP 10 ATTRACTIONS

Cairo 'The city of a thousand minarets' is dusty, noisy and teeming with activity *(page 25)*

A cruise on the Nile Take a *felucca* around the islands at Aswan *(page 72)*

The temples of Luxor and Karnak An avenue of ram-headed sphinxes connects these majestic sites *(pages 49 and 54)*

The Sphinx Guardian of the Khafre's Pyramid at Giza *(page 40)*

The Valley of the Kings See the tombs of the great pharaohs *(page 61)*

The Oases of the Western Desert These form an arc parallel to the Nile *(page 78)*

Mount Sinai An ancient monastery is located at its base *(page 83)*

The Red Sea Stunning coral reefs and exotic fish attract snorkellers and divers *(page 88)*

Alexandria's library This new complex has put the city back on the cultural map *(page 46)*

Abu Simbel Ramesses II's temples reflected the glory of Egypt and his reign, and deterred attackers from the south *(page 75)*

CONTENTS

68

87

35

55

Features

78

94

INTRODUCTION

Egypt's long and illustrious history seems to captivate the modern world. The ancient empire that flourished here from 3200BC until just before the dawn of Christianity was one of the greatest civilisations the world has ever seen. At the beginning of the 19th century, after Napoleon sent his army officers to explore the land and bring back the first hand-drawn impressions of half-buried statues and columns, the Western world couldn't get enough. When Howard Carter peered through the dusty air of Tutankhamun's tomb in 1922 and, in his own words, 'wonderful things' met his eyes, he confirmed the immeasurable wealth of the Pharaohs, and when the backer of the dig, Lord Carnarvon, died suddenly only a few months later, *vox populi* blamed it on the curse of the Pharaoh's mummy – and Hollywood was quick to feed our fantasies. Today, 'pseudo-scientific' theories about the origin and purpose of the pyramids fill the stands of bookshops and the listings on documentary channels. Our interest and curiosity about Egypt is, it seems, insatiable.

Magnificent Sites

People travel to Egypt with a bundle of preconceived ideas, and a sense of excitement. But when it comes to the reality of the archaeological sites, nothing prepares you for their beauty, scale, magnificence and amazing state of preservation. The colossal statues are overwhelming, the delicate grace of the tomb paintings breathtaking, the pyramids prodigious, and the huge temple complexes positively Herculean.

One can see how archaeologists arrive for one season and never leave – the ruins and artefacts, just like the enigmatic smile of the Sphinx, pose more questions than we are able to answer.

The River of Life

Clearly, most visitors are drawn by the mysteries of the ancient world, yet the archaeological sites don't sit in a geographical or cultural vacuum. Egypt in the 21st century is a land of contrasts, but some things never change. Just as in ancient times, without the River Nile, Egypt could not exist. The longest river in the world brings abundant water from the heart of Africa to irrigate a narrow verdant valley snaking its way through the vast Egyptian desert. Its banks are dotted with small villages of modest mud-brick houses surrounded by crops. Ducks waddle in the mud, burdened donkeys tread homewards and oxen till the fields.

The Nile, Egypt's life-blood

A Cultural Mosaic

The people of Egypt give thanks to the Nile, but they worship the common God of Islam and Christianity. The former is the predominant religion: 90 percent of the population is Muslim. The haunting intonations of the *muezzin* drift across the countryside and the cities, calling the faithful to prayer. Egypt also has a Coptic Christian minority, with a history that goes back to St Mark the Evangelist, whose bones were interred in Alexandria until the Venetians carried them off in the year 828. The Copts (the word comes from the

Arabic pronunciation – *qibt* – of the Greek word for Egypt, '*Aegyptios*') are well-integrated into Egyptian society, and have produced leaders in many fields.

Contrasts abound in Egypt. Egyptians are a religious people, but the country is one of the more secular states in the Middle East, with a constitution and judiciary based on Western democratic models instead of *shariah* Muslim religious law. Over 90 percent of its land is uninhabited, yet the major towns and cities are overpopulated. Cairo, the capital, is the largest city in Africa. More than 18 million people live in the dusty, noisy, sprawling, neon-lit metropolis. The majority of its population is, therefore, urban-dwelling, yet many Egyptians still farm the land in the countryside, while the Beduin and Berber tribes live in the oases and the desert. Most Egyptians claim ancient lineage, and although modern religious and social practices have changed, some of the old ways survive. Scenes you see in the countryside today call to mind those exquisite carvings found in the ancient tombs.

Religion and Popular Beliefs

The Egyptian people, both Muslims and Christians, are very pious, and maintain a degree of devoutness that often bewilders Westerners. Religious expressions of a kind that have almost vanished from Western speech proliferate in everyday language. Thus the Arab greeting *As-salam aleikum* (Peace be upon you) is followed by *Aleikum as-salam wa rahmat Allah wa barakatu* (Upon you be peace and the mercy of God and his blessings). *Inshallah* (God willing) is endlessly interjected into any discussion of future plans.

For many Egyptians, belief in the supernatural extends to a world of genies (*djinns*) and spirits of the dead. Fertility rites are still held in Upper Egyptian temples; and magicians, witches and fortune-tellers do a brisk, lucrative trade in spells, amulets and potions.

Egypt's complexity is partly explained by its location at the crossroads of three cultures, between Africa, Europe and the Middle East. It has long been influenced by their differing characteristics, and has assimilated their customs and practices. African gold brought wealth in ancient times, and the darker-skinned Nubians developed trade links with the Ancient Egyptians. Living in the south, around Aswan, the Nubians remain close to their roots and their strong musical traditions.

The invasion of Egypt by Arabs from the east brought a new religion, art and society that swept away much of what had come before. In the 18th and 19th centuries European colonisation left its mark: the *khedives* of Egypt adopted their administrative methods to run the country, and today many Egyptians speak English and French.

Nowadays, it is Cairo, not Thebes, that is the focus of Egypt. Cairo has been the pre-eminent city since the early Muslim era, and the legacy of that time is the city's district of medieval Islamic architecture, which is unrivalled in the world. Powerhouse of the modern economy, Cairo is also the home of the Arab Council and hosts diplomatic talks on the peace process in the Middle East – a crucial role in these uncertain times.

Tourist Attractions

Tourism is the life-blood of the country's economy. An insatiable thirst for history is not the only reason tourists are attracted to Egypt. The seas that lap the arid shores contain pristine marine ecosystems that have lured scuba divers from the inception of the sport. Package tourists soon followed and today the coastline of Egypt is turning

Safety matters

Security measures have increased at Egypt's main archeological sites since the terrorist attacks in Egypt in the 1990s and in New York on 11 September 2001.

Enjoying the gentle pace of life at a camel market

into a year-round seaside playground. With daytime temperatures rarely dropping below about 20°C (the high 60s Fahrenheit) and almost continuous sunshine, it makes a welcome retreat from the drab European winters, and a scorching alternative to temperate summers. The authorities have been quick to respond, allowing hotels and other facilities to develop along the entire Egyptian coastline. Care must now be taken not to blight the fragile environment, particularly the coral reefs in the Red Sea.

Not everything is rosy, of course. With poverty and unemployment rising along with foreign debt, and Islamic fundamentalists who have repeatedly resorted to violence, Hosni Mubarak, the country's president since 1980, has enormous problems to solve. However, with a foot in so many camps – past and present, East and West, religious and secular – Egypt should be well-placed to withstand the vagaries of modern life in the coming years.

A BRIEF HISTORY

Egypt's Nile Valley has supported human life for tens of thousands of years. By 4000BC, the early Egyptians had become farmers of wheat and barley, and a unique civilisation with its own distinctive styles of art and architecture had emerged along the banks of the Nile. The invention of papermaking from papyrus, along with a highly complex system of writing, enabled early Egyptians to keep detailed records and histories at a time when developing cultures in Mesopotamia had to resort to clay tablets for communication.

Ancient Egypt's complicated annals are filled with massive communal building projects and great individuals that can be traced through many millennia. Archaeologists are still debating the exact chronology of certain Egyptian dynasties, but there is general agreement that Egyptian history can be divided into distinct periods, each with a specific name. The Pre-Dynastic and Early Dynastic periods are followed by the Old, Middle, and New Kingdoms with Intermediate periods in between. These are followed by the Late, Macedonian and Ptolemaic periods until Egypt was absorbed into the Roman Empire in the 1st century AD.

Pre- and Early Dynastic Periods (5000–2780BC)

For many years Egypt was not one kingdom but two: Upper Egypt in the south and Lower Egypt in the north. In 3170BC King Narmer of Upper Egypt conquered Lower Egypt. However, the kingdoms were not effectively united until around 3100BC under King Menes – his crown was the first to depict the symbols of both kingdoms. Menes made his capital at Memphis in Lower Egypt (near present-day Cairo), and the First Dynasty was founded. He is also generally thought to have instituted the cult of Ptah, the creator god.

The pyramids served as royal burial places

The Old and Middle Kingdoms

The Old Kingdom was established around 2780BC and lasted more than five centuries. It heralded the first great phase of development in science and architecture; hieroglyphs were developed, and the first great building phase took place.

Rulers looked for ways to prove their might both in life and in death. King Djoser of the Fourth Dynasty was the first to attempt to build a large funerary monument to hold his mortal remains and protect the riches buried with him for his next life. The result is the step pyramid at Saqqarah.

Other rulers followed suit, perfecting the design, and in 2526BC the Great Pyramid at Giza was built for Khufu (or Cheops). Shortly before this, between 2575 and 2550BC, King Chephren had the Sphinx erected in his honour at Giza. It was at about this time that the first mummifications began. Khufu's son Redjedef made a drastic change to Egyptian life when he introduced the solar deity Ra, or Re,

Egyptian mummies

The Ancient Egyptians believed that man was made up of body, *ka* (genius), *ba* (soul) and *akh* (shadow). Upon death these elements were to be reunited to ensure eternal life, hence the need to preserve the body's integrity by mummifying it.

into the Egyptian religion. Worship of Ra became one of the most important facets of Egyptian culture over the next 3,000 years.

Between 2140 and 2040BC, a split occurred between the kingdoms, when rival power bases arose in Heliopolis in Lower Egypt and Thebes (modern Luxor) in Upper Egypt. Archaeologists call this the First Intermediate period. The Karnak temple at Thebes was begun around 2134BC, marking the city's rise to prominence.

The Middle Kingdom, 2040–1801BC, began when the Theban rulers of the 11th Dynasty attempted to extend their control and Egypt was reunified under Mentuhotep II. His successors built a power base at Thebes, and started a cultural renaissance with wide-reaching effects on Egyptian art and archaeology. This was one of the most peaceful and prosperous eras in Ancient Egypt.

In terms of worship, the local Theban god, Amon, became intertwined with Ra creating the deity Amon Ra, and around 1800BC Osiris became a deity. Thebes held onto power until the 12th Dynasty, when its first king, Amenemhet I, who reigned between 1980–1951BC, established a capital near Memphis. However, he continued to pay homage to the Theban god Amon, thereby ensuring that the cult of Amon was observed throughout the kingdom.

The riches of Egypt were coveted by rival peoples and around 1600BC, the Hyksos invaded Lower Egypt from Syria and the desert east of Jordan, and surged southwards, splitting the kingdom in two once again, thereby starting the Second Intermediate period.

The New Kingdom (1540–1100BC)

The rule of the Hyksos lasted less than 100 years. They were driven out of Lower Egypt by Ahmose I who founded the 18th Dynasty, ruling over a united Egypt from the capital of Thebes. The pharaohs of the 18th Dynasty instigated many important reforms. They reorganised the army and consolidated power in the hands of family members at the expense of feudal leaders. Artistically and culturally Egypt reached its zenith during the New Kingdom and many renowned pharaohs reigned during this time. The Valley of the Kings was chosen as a new burial ground for the pharaohs when Tuthmosis I (1504–1492BC) was entombed in a narrow valley across the river from the temple at Karnak.

Throughout the 1400s BC temples and tombs at Karnak and Luxor were greatly expanded and several huge building projects took place on the west bank of the Nile. However, in 1356–39BC a new pharaoh, Amenhotep IV, decided to leave Thebes and, with his wife Nefertiti, created a new capital in the north: Akhétaton (modern Tell al-Amarnah). He introduced a monotheistic cult of the one true god, Aten, and changed his own name to Akhenaten ('He who pleases Aten'). This sudden and radical change caused chaos, and Egypt lost its international influence until Akhenaten's successor – his son, Tutankhamun – reinvested the priests of Amon Ra and his fellow divinites in Thebes.

Akhenaten, dissident pharaoh of the New Kingdom

Tutankhamun died in mysterious circumstances without an heir. His warrior successor, Ramesses I,

Ramesses III, the last of the great Ramesside pharaohs

heralded the start of the 19th Dynasty. His successor, Seti I (1291–1279BC), won back many of the lands lost during the Akhenaten years.

The long rule of Ramesses II (1279–1212BC) came as a great finale to the New Kingdom era. Over an impressive 60 years he supervised magnificent building projects at Luxor and Karnak and commissioned the temple of Abu Simbel. Some scholars now postulate that Ramesses II was the Egyptian pharaoh of biblical fame who allowed the Jews to leave his land for Israel.

Ramesses III tried to follow in the footsteps of Ramesses II by building a vast mortuary complex at Madinat Habu, but power was already slipping from royal hands into those of the priests known as the servants of Amun-Ra. In 1070BC the country was split again, by foreign invaders. The Assyrians dominated Egypt from 715BC and began to develop links with the expanding Roman Empire.

The Ptolemaic Period

In 332BC Alexander the Great conquered Egypt and appointed as governor his Macedonian general, Cleomenes of Naucratis, who was of Greek origin. After Alexander's death in 323BC, power passed to another of Alexander's generals, known as Ptolemy I. The new city of Alexandria, on the Mediterranean coast, became his headquarters as well as the cultural capital of the Hellenistic world, and Thebes finally lost its influence. However, successive Ptolemies were responsible for building and restoring several important temples in Upper Egypt, including Dendarah, Philae and Edfu. They adopted Egyptian gods as their own and did much to promote Egyptian culture rather than simply converting it to Greek.

The Ptolemaic era came to an end with its best-known ruler, Queen Cleopatra. During her lifetime (69–30BC), the queen tried to link her land to Rome, notably through her liaison with Julius Caesar, with whom she had a son, Caesarion. However, destiny turned against Cleopatra with the assassination of Caesar and defeat of Mark Antony in the Battle of Actium; she committed suicide in Alexandria in 30BC. Egypt was reduced to being a province of the Roman Empire, ruled at first from Rome then from Constantinople.

Cleopatra's Charms

The name Cleopatra was given to several of the Ptolemaic princesses, but it is Cleopatra VII (69–30BC) who is the most famous. She came to the throne aged 18, as co-regent with her younger brother Ptolemy XII. Rivalry between them led to her banishment from Egypt, but when Julius Caesar came to Alexandria in 47BC, he took the side of the banished queen and set her on the throne. Soon afterwards Cleopatra bore his only son, Caesarion. Some five years later, after Caesar's assassination, she met Mark Antony. Their legendary love affair brought her three more children but alienated Antony from his supporters in Rome. After his defeat at the naval battle of Actium, Cleopatra was mortally bitten by an asp hidden in a basket of figs.

Although Cleopatra seems to have exerted such a powerful attraction over Julius Caesar and Mark Antony, historians agree that the Egyptian queen was no great beauty; nor was she particularly popular with the Romans, who, when they were not afraid of her, despised her.

The Arab Empire

The first significant wave of Muslim Arab expansion swept over Egypt in AD630, less than 10 years after the death of the prophet Muhammad. His teachings, contained in the Koran, fired the previously disparate tribes of the Arabian peninsula to spread the word of Allah. Egypt became one of the most influential Arab caliphates, particularly from the second half of the 9th century, when it was ruled by the powerful Fatimid dynasty. They established their capital at Al-Qahira ('the Victorious'), which is more familiarly known to Westerners as Cairo.

Roof of the mosque built on part of the temple at Luxor

Over the next two centuries, Cairo became a centre of culture and learning unsurpassed in the Islamic world. The al-Azhar University and mosque were founded during this period. The Fatimid empire was crushed by Saladin in 1169. Flush with victories in the Holy Land over the Crusaders, Saladin established his own dynasty, the Ayyubides, and created a citadel to protect Cairo. But his control was weak, and his power was usurped by the Mamluks, his guard of Turkish slaves, whose dynasty lasted from 1251–1517. They built palaces and mosques and expanded Egypt's trading power, thanks to the market of Khan al-Khalili.

Ottoman Rule

The Mamluks in their turn were overthrown by Ottoman Turks in 1517, but little changed on a day-to-day basis. The Turks effectively left control to a local governor, or pasha, who ran the country as he pleased with Mamluk help. As a result, Egypt went into decline and suffered especially when the Ottoman Empire went into decline in the 18th century.

Napoleon's army stayed in Egypt for only three years

As Ottoman control weakened, Egypt became a pawn in a larger game. In 1798 a young Napoleon Bonaparte, eager to curtail growing British power, invaded Egypt and after a short and decisive battle claimed the country for France. He set about forming a ruling body, and sent scholars and artists out into the countryside to explore and record its ancient treasures – thus sparking the great interest in Egyptology among scholars in France and the rest of Western Europe.

Napoleon's stay in Egypt was short-lived however. The British fleet was after him and inflicted a devastating defeat on the French Navy at the battle of Abu Qir later the same year. Napoleon went home to claim 'victory' but he had to leave behind the bulk of his army.

Meanwhile an Ottoman force had been dispatched from Istanbul to counter the French. They were led by Muhammad Ali, a brilliant intellectual who, in the aftermath of the French withdrawal, asked to be appointed Pasha of Egypt. The Ottoman Sultan agreed to his request. Installed in Cairo, in 1811 Muhammad organised a grand banquet and invited all the notable Mamluks to attend. Once assembled, he had them all massacred. The assassination of their leaders marked the sudden end of the Mamluks' influence in Egypt.

Fascinated by European military strategy, Muhammad Ali set about modernising the army and navy. Attempts were also made to bring agriculture and commerce up to date, and cotton was introduced as a commercial crop. New building projects in Cairo expanded the city's boundaries. Egypt's new ruler grew wealthy and powerful, twice declaring war on his sovereign and almost beating the sizeable but dissolute Ottoman army. Istanbul eventually granted Egypt autonomy and conferred hereditary status on the role of Pasha of Egypt. The title was subsequently upgraded to *khedive* ('king' in Persian, the equivalent of Viceroy).

Muhammad Ali, the founder of modern Egypt

Yet Muhammad Ali's successors lacked their ancestor's talents, and their power was eroded by corruption and irresponsibility. The creation of the Suez Canal, hailed as a marvel of engineering when it opened in 1869, was decided by Khedive Ismail. Yet the enterprise was financed by unscrupulous bankers, and when the *khedive* became overburdened by debt, he had to allow European 'advisers' to control key institutions. The British soon had a tight grip on Egyptian politics and commerce.

The 20th Century

During World War I, Egypt occupied a strategic position for Britain, being close to the Ottoman enemy. In addition, the Suez Canal facilitated access to British dominions in India, the Far East, Australia and New Zealand. When the Ottoman Empire crumbled in the war's aftermath, Egypt declared itself independent, but control of the country remained in London. The

The administrative offices of the Suez Canal

nationalist party eventually gained a majority in the 1920s and became a prominent force in the next few decades.

World War II reaffirmed Egypt's strategic importance, and North Africa became an important field of battle. Axis forces were closing in on Cairo but Allied soldiers stopped them at Al-Alamayn in 1942. Egypt remained in British hands for the rest of the war.

The 1947 UN partition of British Mandate Palestine into an Arab and a Jewish state infuriated the Arab world, which went to war to prevent implementation of the resolution. The nascent state of Israel won an unexpected victory over Egypt in 1948, and three decades of hostilities began.

King Faruq, who had come to the throne in 1936, was seen as a luxury-loving playboy. When he attempted to wrestle control of the Suez Canal from the British, he suffered an embarrassing defeat, both at home and abroad. In July 1952 a group of high-ranking military officers led by Colonel Gamal Abdel Nasser overthrew Faruq and nationalised the Suez Canal. Nasser was to rule for 17 years and, with Soviet aid, Egypt carried out a huge modernisation programme. One

President Hosni Mubarak

key building project was the Aswan High Dam, which provides hydroelectricity and prevents flooding.

Anwar Sadat succeeded Nasser, who died in 1970. Less charismatic and more moderate than his predecessor, he, like Nasser, became embroiled in wars with Israel; these weakened the country and left Sinai in Israeli hands. Part of Sinai was regained by Egypt in the 1973 war and, in the war's aftermath, Sadat launched a diplomatic initiative for which he received a Nobel Peace Prize. In 1979 Egypt negotiated a peace treaty with Israel, despite opposition in the Arab world. Sinai was returned to Egypt, but internal opposition to Sadat's efforts at peace building continued. Sadat was assassinated in 1981.

Current Affairs

President Hosni Mubarak has since worked to secure a place for Egypt at the international negotiation table, hosting a succession of Arab-Israeli peace talks. His pragmatic approach has earned him some admirers, but also a lot of enemies among Egyptian extremists who have repeatedly tried to destabilise his regime. In 1997 gunmen slaughtered 58 tourists and three policemen in Luxor. The instigators were imprisoned, but the tourism industry has taken years to recover. Renewed terrorist bombings on the Sinai peninsula, at Taba in October 2004 and at Sharm al-Shaykh in July 2005, killed around 100 people and once again damaged the tourism industry. However, the vast majority of Egyptians offer tourists as warm a welcome as ever.

Historical Landmarks

Pre-Dynastic Period (until 2780BC) Creation of the 1st dynasty under Menes. Hieroglyphs appear.

Old Kingdom (2780–2040BC) 3rd–4th dynasties. Pyramids built at Saqqarah and Giza.

Middle Kingdom (2040–1540BC) 11th–12th dynasties. Invasion of the Hyksos. New warfare techniques employed.

New Kingdom (1540–1100BC) 18th–20th dynasties. Age of the great pharaohs: Amenhotep I–III, Tuthmosis I–IV, Queen Hatshepsut, Akhenaten, Ramesses I–IX and Tutankhamun. Period of peace and property. Construction of temples at Luxor and of Abu Simbel.

1100–332BC 21st–30th dynasties. Libyan, Nubian, Assyrian, Persian and Greek invasions. Decline and civil war.

Ptolemaic Period (332–30BC) Alexander the Great invades Egypt. Reigns of Ptolemy I–XVI and, lastly, Cleopatra.

Romano-Byzantine Period (30BC–AD639) St Mark introduces Christianity around ad40.

Arab Empire (639–1517) Dynasties of the Umayyads, Abbasids, Fatimids and Ayyubids. From 1250, reign of the Mamluks.

Ottoman Period (1517–1914) Turkish government from Istanbul. Muhammad Ali to power in 1811. Suez Canal opened in 1869.

Protectorate-Monarchy (1914–52) British Protectorate. Monarchy established 1922. King Faruq deposed in July Revolution, 1952.

Republic (1953–70) Gamal Abdel Nasser becomes president. Suez Canal nationalised. Israel invades Sinai. The Six-Day War.

1972 Aswan High Dam completed.

1979 Peace treaty with Israel. Egypt banished from the Arab League.

1981 President Sadat assassinated. Hosni Mubarak succeeds him.

1989 Israel returns Sinai. Egypt rejoins the Arab League.

1997 Massacre of tourists at Luxor. Work begins on the Toshka Canal.

2005 President Mubarak introduces multi-party elections, but still wins with over 80 percent of the votes.

2007 Mubarak puts through unprecedented constitutional reforms.

WHERE TO GO

Egypt covers a million square kilometres (386,000 sq miles), with its population essentially concentrated on the banks of the Nile. Our journey begins in the capital, Cairo, a city that is at once oppressive and bewitching; next come the pyramids of Giza, and the Mediterranean city of Alexandria. Travelling up the Nile we reach the temples of Luxor and Karnak as well as the Theban necropolis. Along the Nile Valley we concentrate on the banks of Lake Nasser, from Aswan to Abu Simbel. After a detour via the oases of the west, our itinerary ends on the banks of the Red Sea and the Sinai peninsula.

CAIRO

Founded in AD641 and expanded by the Fatimids in the 9th century, **Cairo** (Al-Qahira or 'the Victorious') became the most powerful Islamic city of the medieval era, marking the renaissance of Egypt. Located where the Nile valley widens into its delta, it is now the largest city in Africa, with a population of nearly 18 million. The heat, the dust and the noise are constants, and traffic is often at a standstill. Yet Cairo has lots to offer the visitor. Its Egyptian Museum is without rival and its street life a real cultural experience.

Downtown Cairo

Downtown Cairo is the city's modern hub with shopping streets, cafés, restaurants and banks. Much of it was laid out by Khedive Ismail in 1865, inspired by the boulevards of Paris, and European architects designed many of the grand buildings.

The Sphinx stands guard by the Great Pyramid at Giza

Right at its heart is the huge **Maydan at-Tahrir** (Liberation Square), with the Arab League Building, Egypt's centre of bureaucracy the **Mogama'a** and the old **American University of Cairo**. Close by, on the Nile, are the **Nile Hilton**, a landmark for Cairenes and tourists alike, and the magnificent **Egyptian Museum**. East of the square is Qasr an-Nil Street, lined with Western-style shops and restaurants. Nearby is the busy **Maydan Ramesses** with its Victorian railway station fronted by a monumental granite statue of Ramesses II. It is a copy: the original statue, found in Memphis and placed here in 1955, was removed to save it from pollution damage.

Gazirah, the largest island in the Nile, is home to the chic neighbourhood of **Zamalik**. Here the **Gazirah Sporting Club** has facilities for temporary members; while the **Opera House**, which shares a complex with the **Modern Art Museum**, offers less strenuous alternatives. Al-Borg, the **Cairo Tower** (open daily 9am–midnight), provides panoramic views over the city. Designed like a tall lotus, it stands 182m (600ft) high, with a revolving bar-restaurant at the top.

Just across the Galaa Bridge in Giza is the little-visited but splendid **Mr and Mrs Mahmoud Khalil Museum** (open Tues–Sun 9am–5.30pm; admission with passport only). The Khalils' superb 19th- and 20th-century European art collection includes Monet, Picasso, Renoir and Gauguin. The west bank of the Nile is home to **Cairo University** and residential suburbs. **Cairo Zoo** (open daily 9am–6pm) is set in pleasant gardens.

South of Gazirah, **Rawda** island is home to the **Manyal Palace** (open daily 9am–5pm), a museum with royal collections and beautiful gardens, and the **Nilometer**

Arabian Nights

The *Arabian Nights* derive from 15th-century Cairo, described as the 'Mother of the World'; it was a city of wonders where miraculous reversals of fortune were commonplace.

View of Islamic Cairo from the walls of the citadel

(open daily 10am–5pm). The latter was built in AD861 to measure the flood levels of the Nile for taxation purposes. In a small palace in the grounds is the new **Umm Kulthoum Museum** (10am–5pm), which is dedicated to Egypt's most famous singer; there is a small concert hall next door.

Egyptian Museum of Antiquities (Mathaf al-Masri)

Situated on the north side of Tahrir Square, the **Egyptian Museum of Antiquities** (open daily 9am–5.30pm) was built in 1902 as the Cairo Museum. Founded by French architect Auguste Mariette in an attempt to stop the flow of artefacts to museums abroad, it now houses one of the world's major collections and some of Ancient Egypt's finest treasures. The museum is somewhat dated, confusing and often crowded – less so at lunchtime – but with more than 120,000 pieces on display, it is not to be missed. (A new, larger museum is being built near the Giza Pyramids.) The collection will enhance

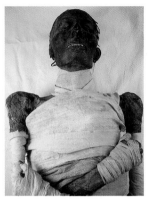

Mummy of Tuthmosis II
in the Egyptian Museum

your understanding and appreciation of Ancient Egypt. Allow at least three hours for the visit – a comprehensive tour will take four or five. Ideally, make one visit before and one after your trips to the Nile temples.

Some of the most famous treasures are on the **second floor**, where objects found at the tomb of Tutankhamun by Howard Carter in 1922 are on display. The only undisturbed royal tomb to be found in the Valley of the Kings, it captured the public imagination. The king was only 19 when he died, and there was little time to prepare a larger tomb, yet it was filled with treasures for use in the afterlife. In the years that followed, the tomb entrance became covered with debris from a nearby tomb, saving it from tomb raiders. Three coffins surrounding the king's mummy are on display. The inner one, made of pure gold, weighs 170kg (374lb). The king's funerary mask in gold and semi-precious stones can also be seen. The awe-inspiring find still dazzles, even after 3,000 years.

In the **Mummy Room** (additional ticket required), also upstairs, you can admire the preserved remains of some of Egypt's most illustrious rulers. Dating mainly from the 18th to the 20th dynasties, they include Ramesses IV, Seti I and Tuthmosis III. Tutankhamun is not among them: the Egyptian authorities decided he should be returned to his tomb in the Valley of the Kings, where he now rests once again in a stone sarcophagus (see page 62).

The **ground floor** rooms follow the chronological history of Ancient Egypt, starting with the magnificent Old Kingdom Rooms. The treasures, mainly found in tombs, include the almost life-size statue of King Zoser discovered near his Step Pyramid at Saqqarah. Rooms 32 and 42 contain further masterpieces, notably the astonishingly lifelike statue of Ka-Aper, carved out of a single piece of wood, and the relaxed, serene statues of couples with their children.

Tomb artefacts are rich sources of clues about daily life and beliefs in Ancient Egypt. The wooden figurines made as servants for the dead included guards, craftsmen and boat crews, complete with their boats, to look after the king in his afterlife. Equally present are images of food sources, such as ducks and cattle, to ensure that the king would be properly provided for in his afterlife.

Funeral masks of Youya and Touya in solid gold

The **Amarnah Room** (Room 3) is devoted to the so-called heretic period when Ahkenaten promoted the worship of one god, the Aten, and founded his capital at Tell al-Amarnah in central Egypt. Ahkenaten's experiment lasted only until his death, when all records of his 'madness' were destroyed. The objects on show were exhumed from his tomb, and include two giant statues of Ahkenaten himself, with his distinctive long chin and rounded belly. There is also a magnificent bust of his wife, Nefertiti.

Among these exquisite and colourful finds are artefacts that enable archaeologists to determine Egypt's chronology. An example is the slate palette of King Narmer, one of the first documents to mention a king, written after Egypt became a unified kingdom.

Statues found throughout the country represent important deities – Osiris, Hathor, Isis and others – and the pharaohs of the major dynasties. The power of the pharaohs is often expressed in the size of their replicas in stone. Thus those of Ramesses II are immense – yet there are also tiny sculptures on display, such as a bust of Queen Hatshepsut.

One of the many statues glorifiying Ramesses II

Islamic Cairo

Although Cairo has many nondescript suburbs, the old districts of al-Qahira are well preserved and contain some of the finest architecture in the Muslim world. Cairo was spared from the annual Nile floods thanks to its location east of the river, and was protected from invaders by a high wall.

Cairo's marketplace, **Khan al-Khalili**, (shops open daily except Sun 10am–7pm, 8pm in summer) still buzzes with the atmosphere of a medieval souk. Narrow alleyways brim with copper, gold, leather and alabaster, and the streets are replete with barrow traders passionately touting for customers. If you search hard enough you can still find magnificent examples of small crafts.

The Khan owes its name to the emir al-Khalili, who built a series of caravanserais or khans for the camel caravans that were the main form of transporting goods at that time. The area around Khan al-Khalili is one of the Middle East's largest marketplaces, and has been so for almost a thousand years. It developed during the Fatimid period between the main city gates of Bab Zuwaylah in the south and Bab al-Futuh in the north.

The architecture lining the streets of Islamic Cairo features exquisite stone carving, delicate woodwork, copper and brasswork and ceramic tiling. Among the many superb buildings that remain from this period are mosques, *madrassas* (religious schools), *khans* and *bayts* (private homes). Of particular note is the **Qalawun, al-Nasir Muhammad and Barquq Mosque Complex** (open daily 9am–6pm), situated on al-Muizz li-Din Allah Street, which was the main artery of Fatimid Cairo. Started in 1285, its long facade is an architectural jewel. The mausoleum of the Mamluk sultan al-Mansur Qalawun, who died in 1290, is at the heart of the complex, surrounded by beautiful Islamic fretwork screens and surmounted by a superb dome.

Next door, the magnificent portal of the **al-Nasir Muhammad madrassa and mausoleum** recalls those of European Gothic churches. In fact, the marble work was part of the booty brought back from a Crusader church in Acre (now Israel) when Arab forces overran it. The **Barquq Mosque** (open daily 9am–5pm) is the youngest in the complex, completed in the late 1300s. Across the road, in the recently restored Sabil-Kuttab of Abd el Rahman Katkhuda (a public fountain with an open-air Koranic school above), a **Museum of Islamic Carpets and Textiles** is scheduled to open.

Continuing towards Bab al-Futuh, a small whitewashed alley, Dar al-Asfar, leads to **Bayt al-Suhaymi** (open daily 9am–5pm), former residence of the rector of the al-Azhar Mosque. Traditional Islamic homes have a large hall, a *qa'a*, which leads to the family rooms as well as to a fountain in the middle. Light enters via a domed roof as the windows are covered by ornate wooden shutters *(mashrabeyas)*.

Balcony of a typical Cairo *bayt*

Centred around a tranquil courtyard, this 18th-century house is an excellent example of Cairene architecture.

Nearby is the **Mosque of al-Hakim**, built in 990 by the Fatimids. One of the city's oldest mosques, it has been much restored by an Ismaili sect from Brunei who venerate the Fatimid Sultan al-Hakim. The symmetry of the large central courtyard has a simple elegance. Plain outer walls give it the look of a fortress rather than a place of worship. The gates that flank it, **Bab al-Futuh** (Gate of Conquest) and **Bab an-Nasr** (Gate of Victory), are part of the recently restored Fatimid **city wall**, which is worth climbing up. Blocks were taken from pharaonic monuments to build the wall, and there are some inscriptions left by Napoleon's soldiers who were garrisoned here.

South of the Khan al-Khalili is Cairo's first Fatimid mosque, the **al-Azhar**, meaning 'The Splendid' (open daily 9am–5pm). Begun in 972, it has been extended considerably over the centuries, and its inner sanctuary now covers 10,360 sq m (4,000 sq ft).

Courtyard of the 14th-century Barquq Mosque

From the outset it was a centre of culture and learning, arguably the first university in the world. It is still the foremost school of Koranic studies, attracting more than 85,000 students per year from Islamic countries.

Just to the west of the al-Azhar is the **al-Ghuri complex** (open daily 9am–5pm), comprising a mausoleum, a mosque, a *madrassa* and a caravanserai. Dating from the start of the 16th century, these elegant monuments were built by the penultimate Mamluk Sultan, Qansuh al-Ghuri. His splendid mausoleum has been under restoration for a few years but should reopen shortly as a cultural centre. Opposite the mausoleum, across what was once the Silk Merchants' Bazaar, is the splendidly restored **al-Ghuri Mosque**, and around the corner is the **Wikalat al-Ghuri**, an old caravanserai now used as a crafts centre, with workshops for local artists.

Walk south along the busy market street that crosses the al-Ghuri complex to reach **Bab Zuwaylah**, the southern entrance to the old city. Its beautifully restored round bastions support the ornate minarets of the **al-Muayyad Mosque**, built in 1420, and frame a tiny gate that was used as a permanent scaffold to hang criminals.

From the gate go west (right) along Ahmed Mahir street to the **Museum of Islamic Art**, or Mathaf al-Islami (open daily 9am–4pm, closed for restoration at the time of writing), inaugurated in 1903. Its superb collection is assembled in several rooms each devoted to a separate skill, such as wood carving, ivory work and the writing of manuscripts. Elaborately decorated arms are also on display.

The Citadel (al-Qal'a; open daily 9am–5pm, 6pm in summer) is a 30-minute walk or 10-minute taxi ride south of the al-Azhar, with the entrance on Salah Salem Road. Built on high ground in the early 13th century, the massive fortification was designed to protect the city from Crusaders. Later it became the palace of the Mamluks, and it was a British garrison during World War II. The size of a small village, the site now houses mosques, museums and cafés. It is from here that the canon is fired to mark the end of the Ramadan fast. The centrepiece of the citadel is the **Muhammad Ali Mosque**, built between 1824 and 1857. The largest mosque in the city, it has earned the name 'Alabaster Mosque' for its grand interior faced with smooth pale stone. The inner sanctuary hall is a monumental space in Ottoman Turkish style, surmounted with a series of beautifully painted domes. The tomb of Muhammad Ali sits under the colonnade, with a facade

The Ottoman Turkish-style Muhammad Ali Mosque

Shimmering interior of the 'Alabaster Mosque'

of intricately sculpted marble. Nearby is the much simpler **al-Nasir Mosque**, sharing Persian and Mongol influences.

Just north of the citadel is the **al-Azhar Park** (daily 8am–10pm), a wonderful Aga Khan Trust project that transformed an enormous rubbish dump into a much needed green zone in one of Cairo's poorest areas. The park has several water features and a few excellent restaurants; it commands sweeping views over the old Fatimid city.

Also nearby, **Maydan Salah ad-Din** is lined with grand mosques, the most beautiful of which is the splendid **Madrassa of Sultan Hasan** (open daily 8am–5pm, 6pm in summer), a masterpiece from 1362. Four separate schools are arranged around its large central courtyard, each with its own portal and inner courtyard. The minaret on the southwest corner is the tallest in Cairo at 81m (265ft). To the right of the *madrassa* is the **Rifa'i Mosque**, completed in 1902, containing the tombs of the descendants of Muhammad Ali, and

Typical decorative motif found in the Citadel

that of the last Shah of Iran, who died in 1980.

A short walk west from the Sultan Hasan *madrassa* leads to the **Mosque of Ibn Tulun** (open daily 8am–6pm), founded in 876 in a military compound established by Ibn Tulun who became governor of Egypt in 868. The beautiful, simple mosque is unusual in Cairo in that it has no facade – it is hidden behind a protective wall with some 19 openings. It also has the only spiral minaret in the city. Behind the mosque, the **Gayer-Anderson Museum** (open daily 8am–4pm) contains outstanding Islamic and European furniture, art and handicrafts. Built as a private residence in 1540 and amalgamated with an adjacent house (Bayt al-Kritliya) dating from 1631, it was bought by the British major Robert Gayer-Anderson in the 1930s. He completely restored the building, filling it with his own collections of antiquities and art works acquired while travelling in the region.

Old Cairo

South of the city centre, **Old Cairo** (Masr al-Qadima) was built on the Roman fortress of Babylon-in-Egypt. Newly restored, it is the heartland of Cairo's important Coptic community. The Coptic church was established in the early years of Christianity, and today almost 10 percent of Egyptians are Copt. The easiest way to reach Old Cairo is to take metro line 1 south from Tahrir Square to the Mar Girgis stop.

Once there were more than 20 churches in this small, peaceful enclave, but only a few survive today. The enclave is entered through one of the old Roman gates. The 7th-century **al-Muallaqah** or 'Hanging Church' (open daily 8am–4pm; Coptic Mass Fri 8–11am, Sun 9–11am) derives its name from its location between two towers of the Roman gate. With foundations dating from the 4th century AD it could be the oldest church in Egypt. Nearby **Abu Serga Church** (St Sergius) also claims this distinction; it is said to have been built at the site where Joseph, Mary and the infant Jesus took shelter after fleeing to Egypt from the Holy Land.

The **Church of St Barbara**, decorated in a typically Coptic style, is also worth visiting. On the left you pass a gate which once marked the entrance to the Jewish quarter. The **Synagogue Ben-Ezra** (open 9am–4pm), beautifully restored with funds from the US, is now no longer used for regular services.

Housed in an old palace, a prime attraction in Old Cairo is the **Coptic Museum** (open daily 9am–5pm). Its collection covers all aspects of Coptic art and worship, from vestments, tapestries, early handwritten Bibles and painted icons, to ornate stone niches and wood-carved ceilings taken from churches and monasteries all over Egypt. These artefacts illustrate the development from Ancient Egyptian to Christian art.

Coptic Museum textile exhibit

THE PYRAMIDS (AL-AHRAM)

Giza

The pyramids of Egypt have exerted a powerful hold on the world since explorers first began to examine this ancient land in detail. Were they simply tombs for pharaohs, or astronomical markers to aid the quantifying of time; or were they built to concentrate a natural energy source? More outlandish theorists posit that the pyramids were not built by humans at all, speculating that they are a sign of an alien intelligence, which visited the earth thousands of years ago.

Camels for hire at the Great Pyramid

Whatever the latest theory, the **Pyramids of Giza** (the best known) are without doubt extremely impressive monuments. Their sandstone facades reflect the sunlight: rose-coloured in the morning, golden in the heat of the day, and smoky purple as night falls. It is impossible not to marvel at the feat of engineering and organisation that resulted in millions of stone blocks being transported to the site and placed precisely one atop another, all without the aid of power tools or lifting equipment.

Archaeologists agree that the Giza pyramids were built within a few hundred years of each other around 2600BC by generations of the same

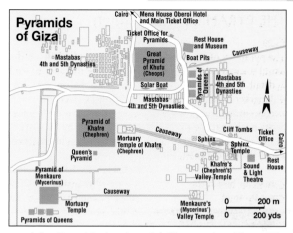

Pyramids of Giza

Cairo / Mena House Oberoi Hotel and Main Ticket Office

Ticket Office for Pyramids

Rest House and Museum

Causeway

Mastabas 4th and 5th Dynasties

Great Pyramid of Khufu (Cheops)

Boat Pits

Solar Boat

Pyramids of Queens

Mastabas 4th and 5th Dynasties

Mastabas 4th and 5th Dynasties

N

Pyramid of Khafre (Chephren)

Causeway

Cliff Tombs

Ticket Office

Cairo

Queen's Pyramid

Mortuary Temple of Khafre (Chephren)

Sphinx

Sphinx Temple

Sound & Light Theatre

Rest House

Pyramid of Menkaure (Mycerinus)

Khafre's (Chephren's) Valley Temple

Causeway

Mortuary Temple

Menkaure's (Mycerinus') Valley Temple

Pyramids of Queens

0   200 m

0   200 yds

royal family, with the aim of foiling tomb robbers. The largest of the three, the **Great Pyramid of Khufu**, is the only survivor of the Seven Wonders of the World described by Greek and Roman scholars. It stands 137m (450ft) high and was the tallest structure in the world until 1889 when the Eiffel Tower was built in Paris. Originally covered with a smooth layer of polished limestone and capped with a gleaming pyramidion, it would have reflected sunlight like a beacon across the Nile valley. The interior contrasts strongly with the vast exterior. Steep, narrow tunnels lead to a tiny funerary chamber containing a simple granite sarcophagus. More remarkable is the ventilation system: astronomers have proved that the air shafts are aligned with major constellations in the skies of Ancient Egypt.

The **Pyramid of Khafre** is smaller than the Great Pyramid, though its location on slightly higher ground makes it appear taller. A red granite sarcophagus was found in the interior chamber. The smallest pyramid, **Menkaure**, adds a wonder-

Emerging from the Great Pyramid of Khufu

ful perspective to the alignment of the three pyramids. To the south are three smaller pyramids thought to be for the family of Menkaure.

The three pharaohs were not the only ones laid to rest at Giza, which was the site of a royal burial ground from the days of the Old Kingdom. The desert landscape is dotted with mud-brick tombs and *mastabas* (stone tombs with flat roofs), though they are certainly not as impressive as the pyramids themselves.

Seated at the base of the sacred causeway that once linked the pyramid of Khafre to the Nile is the **Sphinx**, the enigmatic depiction of Khafre with his head attached to a lion's body. In Egyptian mythology, sphinxes were guardian deities, and this was monumental protection, being 73m (240ft) long and 20m (66ft) high. Following Khafre's death, the body of the Sphinx was progressively buried by desert sand. Tuthmosis IV believed that the statue spoke to him, telling him he would become pharaoh if he cleared the sand away – which he hastened to do. From then on, ancient Egyptians believed that the monument possessed prophetic powers.

Behind the Great Pyramid of Khufu is the **Solar Boat Museum** (open daily 9am–5pm), housing the beautifully restored cedar longboat thought to have brought the body of the dead pharaoh from the east to the west bank of the Nile.

You can tour the pyramids (open daily 8am–4pm, 5pm in summer) on foot, or take a camel or horseback ride between the main sites. Access to the interior of Khufu is limited to 150 in the morning and 150 from 1pm.

Saqqarah

Giza was neither the first or the only location where pyramids were built: there are about 90 built along the Nile between Giza and the oasis of al-Fayoum. The oldest pyramid is at Saqqarah, situated about an hour south of Cairo.

Saqqarah was the final resting place for the rulers of Memphis and constitutes the largest royal graveyard in Egypt. Dominating the area is the **Step Pyramid**, built by architect Imhotep for his ruler King Zoser in about 2670BC, and made up of six brick tiers, reaching a height of 60m (196ft). Inside, a shaft was dug 28m (91ft) to the king's burial chamber. The pyramid is surrounded by a compound representing the king's palace at Memphis, with beams, columns and bundles of reeds carved onto its facade. Several tombs

Saving the Sphinx

Although it was cleared of desert sand many times in antiquity, the Sphinx remained protected by the sand for several centuries. Until the day when the Mamluks, judging the statue's smile too 'pagan' for their liking, removed its nose and beard using cannon fire. The nose has never been found, but the beard is now in London's British Museum, which refuses to return it to its owner.

As if this mutilation was not enough, in 1987 a team of scientists discovered the alarming presence of a sheet of water under the paws of the unfortunate Sphinx. A year later, a 200-kg (450-lb) chunk detached itself from the right shoulder. The Sphinx was then submitted to disgraceful patching up with cement. Fortunately, recent restoration work has been carried out using limestone rock similar to the original. Studies have shown that the head and neck are made of hard stone, but the body is porous and friable, and so extremely vulnerable to wind erosion. Researchers agree on the main causes of the Sphinx's deterioration: wind erosion, pollution and mass tourism.

Earliest of them all: the Step Pyramid at Saqqarah, c.3000BC

surrounding the pyramid are decorated with extremely fine murals. Notable examples are the scenes of nobles hunting, feasting and fishing in the **tombs of Kagemni and Mereruka** (2300BC), next to the ruined pyramid of Teti. Doctors are shown performing operations in the tomb of Ankh-ma-hor. Near the Rest House and the now-closed Serapeum, the double *mastaba* **of Akhet-hotep** and his son **Ptah-hotep** contains scenes from daily life in Ancient Egypt, including various children's games. Across the road is the *mastaba* **of Ti**, decorated with fish and birds. The *mastaba* **of Princess Idut** has exceptional nautical scenes.

Just southeast of Saqqarah is **Memphis** (open daily 8am–5pm), capital of Egypt until the end of the 6th Dynasty (c.2200BC). Little remains of the city now – the two major relics are a monumental statue of Ramesses II lying prostrate after losing its feet, and an alabaster sphinx dating from 1400BC.

ALEXANDRIA & MEDITERRANEAN COAST

There are two roads from Cairo to Alexandria. One leads through the fertile lands of the Nile Delta, past orchards and fields of cotton and rice. Life seems to have changed little in generations, apart from the arrival of electricity in the mud-brick houses. The second route passes through the desert to the west of Cairo towards **Wadi Natrun**, an important region in Ancient Egypt because it was the main source of natron, the mineral used in mummification and in glassmaking.

In the 4th century AD, to escape Roman persecution, Coptic Christians founded a large community here dedicated to prayer and contemplation. Four monasteries remain, each with a church, monks' quarters and a sturdy surrounding wall. The most important, **Deir Abu Makar** (St Makarios), provided several Coptic popes. Nearby **Deir Anba Bishoi** and **Deir as-Suriani** were both founded by St Bishoi, but the latter was bought in the 8th century by wandering Syrian monks. **Deir al-Baramous** was the most isolated of the monasteries before the road was built; its oldest church, the Church of the Virgin, contains 13th-century wall frescoes.

Alexandria

Founded by Alexander the Great on the Mediterranean coast in 322BC, **Alexandria** was capital of Egypt during the Ptolemaic era. It had sumptuous palaces and temples, and the ancient world's best known library. Ships from all over the Mediterranean docked at the double harbour, where the entrances were protected by the **Pharos Lighthouse**, one of the Seven Wonders of the

Beacon of light

Built in AD279, the Pharos lighthouse was 135m (440ft) high with an enthroned statue of Poseidon at the summit. It was the only Wonder of the World to have a practical purpose.

World. Unfortunately, all this splendour was lost in a series of earthquakes at the start of the first millennium. Much of ancient Alexandria now rests below the harbour waters. Recent underwater excavations have revealed a wealth of blocks and statuary just metres below the surface of the Eastern Harbour.

Despite the earthquakes, Alexandria continued to develop. The port was the main entry point into Egypt until the advent of air travel in the early 20th century. Its trading contacts with the outside world made it Egypt's most cosmopolitan city. Numerous European and British expatriots stayed here in the late 19th and early 20th centuries, and their lifestyles were portrayed by Lawrence Durrell in his work, *The Alexandria Quartet*. The 1952 coup marked the end of this 'little Europe' but there remains a certain colonial atmosphere.

The city sits on a wide bay lined with colonial buildings that find their full splendour at sunset. Myriad fishing boats bob in the water, bringing their catches to the restaurants of the **Corniche**. The western end of the bay sweeps round to a headland where the Pharos Lighthouse once stood. Today the 15th-century **Fort of Qayt Bay** (open daily 9am–4pm) occupies the site. Part of the fort is a **Marine Museum**, with aquariums holding species from the Red Sea and Mediterranean. West is the **Palace of Ras al-Tin**, built for Muhammad Ali in 1834. It was here that King Faruq abdicated in 1952 before setting sail for exile in Italy.

The Fort of Qayt Bay offers a superb view of Alexandria

The way back to the town centre along the corniche is a pleasant stroll. On the way, the **Mosque of Abu al-Abbas**

The magnificent Mosque of Abu al-Abbas al-Mursi at dusk

al-Mursi is worth a look (women are only allowed access to the back part). Rebuilt in 1943, it holds the tomb the 13th-century sheikh Abu al-Abbas. The Moorish stonework is exquisite and the domes and minaret remarkably elegant.

The small square of **Maydan Zaghlul** on the seafront marks the centre of town and is very busy at rush hour. On its west side, **Cecil Hotel** was the meeting place of glitterati in colonial times. A short walk from here, just off Safiya Zaghlul street, is the **Greco-Roman Museum** (open 9am–5pm, closed Fri 11.30am–1.30pm; closed for restoration at the time of writing), with its collection of Greek, Roman and Ptolemaic objects found locally. The **Alexandria National Museum** (open 9am–4pm) on al-Hurriya Street relates the city's distinct history through objects found in the city, often taken from other museums. Exhibits are well presented, arranged chronologically over three floors. Of particular interest is the sphinx and other sculptures found during underwater excavations.

Near the train station are the excavations of **Kom al-Dikkah** (open daily 9am–5pm), where a Polish mission has found a Roman residential area, baths and a small 2nd-century theatre with beautiful mosaic flooring. Some statues discovered in the Eastern Harbour are also on display here.

A walk, or a short taxi ride, to the southwest are the impressive **catacombs of Kom as-Shuqafah** (open daily 9am–5pm). Dating from the 2nd century AD, the tombs are decorated in a typical Alexandrian blend of classical and Egyptian styles.

A few minutes' walk to the northeast is **Pompey's Pillar** (Al-Amud as-Sawari). Made of red granite, the 30-m (95-ft) column was raised to honour Emperor Diocletian, not the Roman general after whom it is named. This is all that remains of Rhakotis, the spiritual centre of ancient Alexandria.

Facade of the new Alexandria Library, opened in 2002

Here too was the **ancient library of Alexandria**, founded by Ptolemy I, and one of the biggest of its time, comprising some 70,000 works. It was damaged by several fires then completely destroyed by the Arab invasion of 640. At the dawn of the 21st century the government decided to create a library worthy of its predecessor. With the help of UNESCO, the ultra-modern **Biblioteka Alexandrina** (open Sat–Thur 11am–7pm and Fri 3–7pm; <www.bib

alex.org>) was constructed along the coast road east of Maydan Zaghlul square. Inaugurated in 2002, the library's façade, in grey Aswan granite, is covered with inscriptions of all the known alphabets. The complex includes a **Manuscript Museum**, **Culturama** (an interactive show on Egypt's history), a **Planetarium** and an **Antiquities Museum**.

The cemetery of Al-Alamayn

There is no beach in the centre of Alexandria, but the resort of **Muntazah**, 8km (5 miles) to the east, offers sand, sea and hotels. **Muntazah Palace**, built in the 19th century, is now a smart hotel-casino surrounded by beautiful gardens.

The Mediterranean Coast

West of Alexandria, desert predominates, except along the coast where there was a building boom in the late 1990s. Where only recently there were virgin beaches, now mile upon mile of concrete holiday resorts catering mainly for Egyptians line the strand until **Al-Alamayn**, a 90-minute drive along the coast.

This tiny desert railway crossing was the scene of one of the pivotal battles of World War II, in which Allied soldiers defeated Rommel's German and Italian forces in 1942. In the cemetery shared by the casualties of both armies engaged in the historic battle, a monument now stands as a poignant memorial. There is also a small **museum** here with uniforms, military hardware and maps illustrating the battle plans and tactics of this most gruelling theatre of war.

MAIN SITES IN THE NILE VALLEY

The land of Upper Egypt, in the south of the country, is so-named because it is upriver of Cairo and the Nile Delta area (known as Lower Egypt). Upper Egypt was the heartland of the Ancient Egyptian kingdom at the peak of its power, and the remains of its ancient cities form one of the most important and breathtaking archaeological collections in the world.

Luxor

The capital of Upper Egypt, Luxor is a key site for Egyptology. Today's city is a modern agglomeration situated on the east bank of the Nile some 800km (500 miles) from Cairo. Its name in Arabic – al-Uqsor – means 'the palaces', indicating the importance of this area in Ancient Egypt. Known as Thebes by the ancient Greeks, Luxor was Egypt's capital city and religious centre for centuries, reaching its peak in the New Kingdom era (c.1540–1100BC). By the time the Romans arrived it was already well into decline, which began with the Assyrian invasion in the 7th century BC and the departure of the Ptolemies for Alexandria three centuries later. Sand progressively invaded the city, eventually burying it. The Arab town was built on top, covering ancient treasures buried below. Luxor's major his-

Avenue of the Sphinxes

toric monuments have been cleared of sand over the past century. On the west bank are the remains of mortuary temples and, more importantly, the tombs of the great pharaohs of Egypt, hidden in a valley beyond the fertile river plain. The city's new governor plans to make Luxor the world's largest open-air museum, and much work is being done to clean up all the historical sites as well as the city centre.

The Temple of Luxor

In the heart of town, beside the Nile, is the **Temple of Luxor** ◄ (open 6am–9pm, 10pm in winter), largely built by Amenhotep III in the 18th Dynasty (*c.*1350BC) and embellished by Ramess-

es II in the 19th Dynasty. The temple was the home of Amun-Ra's wife, mother goddess Mut, and son, moongod Khonsu. Amun-Ra resided in Karnak, but for the festival of Opet (new year) his statue was brought here to be with his family.

Before reaching the temple, admire the splendid 4th-century BC **Avenue of Ram-Headed Sphinxes**, which connects with the Karnak Temple *(see page 54)* to the north. Opposite the temple's great pylon (entrance) are majestic statues of Ramesses II and a large granite obelisk – one of an original pair. The other, presented to France in 1831 by Muhammad Ali, stands in Paris' Place de la Concorde.

Only one of the two obelisks remains at the temple entrance

Entering the **Great Court of Ramesses II**, you see perched on top of the hall the **Mosque of Abu al-Haggag**, protecting the tomb of a 12th-century holy man. The mosque and tomb were part of the small town built over the sand-covered temple. The entrance to the mosque is through a door in the east wall above the temple.

Beyond the court is the **Grand Colonnade of Amenhotep III**, with massive papyrus-bud columns, which were the prototype for the Great Hypostyle Hall at Karnak *(see page 54)*. The walls were decorated during the reign of Tutankhamun with scenes of the great Opet Festival that took place every year. The west wall represents the procession from Karnak to Luxor temple, and the better-preserved east wall depicts the return journey. This leads to the **Sun Court of Amenhotep III** where a cache of statues was found in 1989, now in the Luxor Museum *(see below)*. Wall carvings depict Amenhotep making offerings to the gods in thanks for his divine power.

Detail from a relief in the Sun Court of Amenhotep III

Along the Corniche

Between the Temple of Luxor and the Nile is the **Corniche** (officially the Shari an-Nil), a tree-lined avenue leading to the town. A wide path follows the river bank, ideal for a shady stroll. The *felucca* (Nile sailboat) captains gather here, looking out for tourists. Further on, Nile cruisers disgorge their passengers for tours or shopping trips. Horse-drawn carriages ply the Corniche offering trips to Karnak, or a ride back to your hotel.

Also on the Corniche, on the same side of the river, is the **Mummification Museum** (open daily 9am–1pm and 4–9pm, 5–10pm in summer), which explains the complete mummification process. To the north, the modern **Archaeological Museum of Luxor** (open daily 9am–1pm and 4–9pm, 5–10pm in summer) is well conceived, and will complement your visit to the surrounding temples. Look out for the basalt statue of Tuthmosis III. Behind the Mosque of Abu al-Haggag is the busy **souk**. Before buying pottery or alabaster, compare prices and quality with goods on sale at the west bank's artisan villages.

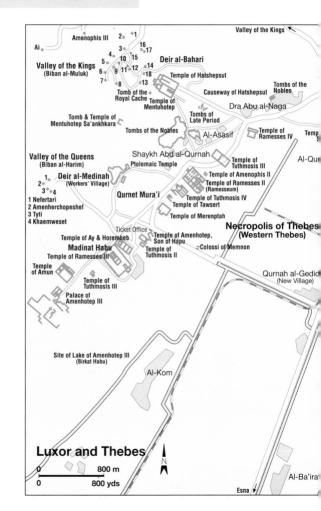

Valley of the Kings

Amenophis III

Ai

Valley of the Kings
(Biban al-Muluk)

Deir al-Bahari

Temple of Hatshepsut

Tombs of the
Nobles

Tomb of the
Royal Cache

Temple of
Mentuhotep

Causeway of Hatshepsut

Dra Abu al-Naga

Tombs of
Late Period

Tomb & Temple of
Mentuhotep Sa'ankhkara

Tombs of the Nobles

Al-Asasif

Temple of
Ramesses IV

Temp

Shaykh Abd al-Qurnah

Valley of the Queens
(Biban al-Harim)

Ptolemaic Temple

Temple of
Tuthmosis III

Al-Qur

Deir al-Medinah
(Workers' Village)

Temple of Amenophis II
Temple of Ramesses II
(Ramesseum)

1 Nefertari
2 Amenherchopeshef
3 Tyti
4 Khaemweset

Qurnet Mura'i

Temple of Tuthmosis IV
Temple of Tawsert

Temple of Merenptah

Ticket Office

Necropolis of Thebes
(Western Thebes)

Temple of Ay & Horemheb

Temple of Amenhotep,
Son of Hapu

Madinat Habu

Temple of
Tuthmosis II

Colossi of Memnon

Temple of Ramesses III

Temple
of Amun

Qurnah al-Gedid
(New Village)

Temple of
Tuthmosis III

Palace of
Amenhotep III

Site of Lake of Amenhotep III
(Birkat Habu)

Al-Kom

Luxor and Thebes

N

0 ———— 800 m
0 ———— 800 yds

Al-Ba'ira

Esna

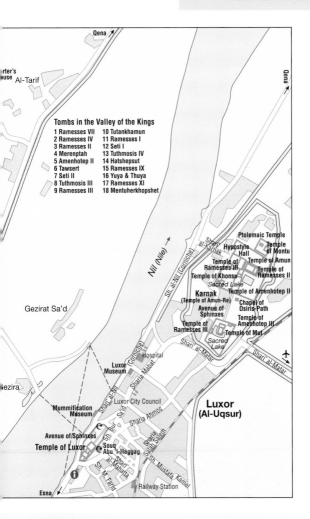

Tombs in the Valley of the Kings

1 Ramesses VII	10 Tutankhamun
2 Ramesses IV	11 Ramesses I
3 Ramesses II	12 Seti I
4 Merenptah	13 Tuthmosis IV
5 Amenhotep II	14 Hatshepsut
6 Tawsert	15 Ramesses IX
7 Seti II	16 Yuya & Thuya
8 Tuthmosis III	17 Ramesses XI
9 Ramesses III	18 Mentuherkhopshet

Qena

Al-Tarif

rter's
use

Nil (Nile)

Sh. al-Nil (Corniche)

Gezirat Sa'd

Qena

Ptolemaic Temple
Shari al-Karnak
Hypostyle Hall
Temple of Montu
Temple of Ramesses III
Temple of Amun
Temple of Khonsu
Temple of Ramesses II
Sacred Lake
Karnak (Temple of Amun-Re)
Temple of Amenhotep II
Avenue of Sphinxes
Chapel of Osiris-Path
Temple of Ramesses III
Temple of Amenhotep III
Sacred Lake
Temple of Mut

Shari al-Matar

Hospital

Shari al-Nil (Corniche)

Luxor Museum

Sharia Mabat

ezira

Shari al-Nil Sa'id

Luxor City Council

Mummification Museum

Sharia Ahmos

Avenue of Sphinxes

Luxor (Al-Uqsur)

Shari al-Matar

Temple of Luxor

Sh. Bur Sa'id

Souq Abu 'l-Haggag

Sharia al-Mahata

Sh. M. Farid

Sh. Sh. Mustafa Kamel

Sharia Salom

Esna

Railway Station

Karnak

The **Temple of Karnak** (open 6.30am–5.30pm in winter, 6am–6pm in summer) lies 2km (1½ miles) from the centre of Luxor. At the height of Theban power, Karnak was known as Ipet-Isut, 'the Most Perfect of Places'. Begun during the Old Kingdom, it became the national shrine from the 11th Dynasty, *c.*2134BC. The temple complex was expanded during the following centuries, with each pharaoh adding his own shrines and monuments. The Amun temple enclosure alone covered 260,000 sq metres and over 80,000 people worked for the temple. Karnak was abandoned around the 4th century AD when the Egyptians turned to Christianity.

The **Avenue of the Ram-Headed Sphinxes** marks the route from the Nile to the temple entrance. This was used for ceremonies, when statues of the gods were carried to the river

The entire temple complex at Karnak is dedicated to Amun

for journeys to the west bank, or to the Luxor sanctuary. The ram was the sacred animal of the god Amun.

The temple is entered through a colossal pylon, one of the most recent structures on the site and, though never actually finished, the largest to be built in Egypt during the Ptolemaic period.

The Karnak temple complex extends over 3 sq km (1 sq mile). At its heart is the **Temple of Amun**, most powerful of the Theban gods. The gateway leads to

Dense forest of giant columns in the Hypostyle Hall

an immense temple courtyard, the largest in Egypt. To the left is the diminutive **Temple of Seti II**, and further along on the right a larger **temple dedicated to Ramesses III**.

A second smaller pylon, fronted by statues of Ramesses II, shields Karnak's masterpiece, the **Great Hypostyle Hall**. Its 134 immense columns recreate the papyrus forests of the sacred island from which all life sprang. This mighty work, the largest hall of any temple in the world, was started by Amenhotep III. Seti I (1291–78BC) decided to complete it, a task finally left to his son Ramesses II, who placed the appropriate colossi of himself at the entrance. The northern walls are decorated with remarkable bas-reliefs of Seti I's battles in Syria and Lebanon.

Behind the third pylon is one of the two obelisks raised by Tuthmosis III, still standing. Beyond the fourth pylon is the oldest preserved part of the temple constructed by Tuthmosis III around the splendid obelisks erected by his stepmother Hatshepsut. Her pink granite obelisk is the tallest in Egypt, measuring 30m (97ft) high. Originally the point was topped by a cap of pure gold, which reflected the sun and acted as a beacon. Her other obelisk lies near the sacred lake. Further along is the sacred boat shrine, built by Alexander the Great in 332BC.

Beyond the main temple complex, Karnak stretches as far as the eye can see, but many remains are difficult to identify. An interesting building towards the rear is the **Festival Hall of Tuthmosis III**, a stone reproduction of the field tent the pharaoh used on his many military campaigns, with the central row of columns higher than those at the edge in order to support an imaginary canvas. During his reign Tuthmosis extended the Egyptian empire from Syria to the Sudan.

South of the temple, the **Sacred Lake** was used for ceremonies. Today it forms the setting for the second part of the Sound and Light Show.

The giant granite **scarab** to the northwest of the lake is worth a look. Originally it was placed in front of the temple of Amenemhet III on the west bank. Egyptians claim it brings you luck if you walk three times counter-clockwise around the scarab before touching it and making a wish.

Egyptian Temples

Although no two Egyptian temples are identical, they were all built according to the same plan. A monumental gateway, or pylon, led to a courtyard that was open to the sky; a second pylon opened onto another courtyard; then there was a 'hypostyle' hall, its ceiling supported by columns. A vestibule led to the 'offering court', then to the inner parts of the temple and finally to the sanctuary, which was quite dark. Only the pharaoh and the priests were allowed into this 'holy of holies', where a gold-plated image of the presiding god was kept.

The Temple of Hatshepsut

Thebes

Although they ruled from palaces on the east bank of the Nile, the pharaohs chose to be buried on the west bank, the last resting place of the god Amun Ra, symbolised by the setting sun. Tuthmosis I was the first pharaoh to be entombed there, *c.*1490BC, choosing a narrow valley away from the capital where the secret resting place cut deep into the rock would protect him after his death. Others followed his example, creating a veritable 'city of the dead' with each tomb more elaborate or brightly decorated than the last.

Although the Valley of the Kings is the best known, it is not the only attraction on the west bank of the Nile. There are temples, towns and hundreds of lesser tombs, known collectively as the **Necropolis of Thebes**.

From the ferry docking station the road leads to the low hills that hide the tombs. Two huge stone sentinels stand watch over the plain, facing the Nile. These are the statues of

A fine and remarkably
well-preserved bas-relief

Amenhotep III, the **Colossi of Memnon**; from a height of 21m (68ft) they once guarded the entrance to his funerary temple, but they are all that remain. The **ticket office** for all the sites is just past the Colossi of Memnon, at the crossroads (the system is changing so tickets are sold at each site, but check at the office first). The sites are open daily, 6am–7pm in summer, 7am–5pm in winter.

Where the road divides, the road straight ahead leads to the **Valley of the Queens**, and the road to the left goes to the temple complex of **Madinat Habu**. Often left out of the tour-group itinerary, this part of the west bank is much quieter and it offers interesting insights into Egyptian life and superb archaeological remains. Queens and royal children were buried in a valley separate from their husbands and fathers. The renowned Theban queen Nefertari, wife of Ramesses II, has the most ornate tomb (No. 66), but access is limited to VIP groups only.

Below the Valley of the Queens are the remains of the town of the artisans, called **Deir al-Medinah**, home to generations of painters, masons and builders who worked on the royal tombs. Simple brick homes stand row upon row and a wealth of everyday artefacts was found here, notably cooking utensils and work tools. Also excavated were simple tombs where the artisans buried their dead. Those of **Sennedjem** (No. 1) and **Inherka** (No. 359) are worth exploring.

A right turn at the junction leads along the valley floor past the modern artisan village of **Shaykh Abd al-Gurnah**, known for its alabaster and onyx objects. The simple brick buildings faced with ochre and blue stucco, though larger than those at Deir al-Medinah, are similar in style. Here, too, tombs and temples are scattered in the fields, the oldest being the **Ramesseum**, the mortuary temple of Ramesses II. Built to hold ceremonies during his visits from Thebes, the Ramesseum was decorated with majestic statues of the pharaoh, and the pylon depicts him triumphant at the Battle of Qadesh, when he quashed the Hittites. Sadly, much of the temple lies in ruins.

The village of Gurna, on the opposite side of the road, was destroyed in order to avoid further water damage to the **Tomb of the Nobles**. The most beautiful of these tombs date from the 18th Dynasty when Egyptian art and creativity were at their peak. The **Tomb of Nakht** (No. 52), a temple astronomer, is worth a look. The wall paintings depict the Nile at its most splendid, with abundant fruit, as well as wine-making scenes. The nearby **Tomb of Menna** (No. 69) contains realistic scenes

A wealth of themes was used to decorate the tombs' walls

of harvesting and threshing. The **Tomb of Khaemhat** (No. 57) was decorated with statues of himself and his family – very rare for tombs of his class. The **Tomb of Ramosis** is also interesting: a high official in the court of Amenhotep IV, he began to prepare an elaborate resting place decorated with fine bas-reliefs, but had to abandon it, unfinished, when he followed his master to the new capital, Tell al-Amarnah.

Before turning off the coastal plain into the Valley of the Kings, one of the most impressive Theban temples comes into view on the left, that of Queen Hatshepsut. A remarkable woman, she ruled as coregent with her brother, Tuthmosis II, and then her stepson, Tuthmosis III. The **Temple of Hatshepsut** (Deir al-Bahari), dedicated to the goddess Hathor, is a vast three-tiered structure, carved into the base of the rose-coloured hillside, facing out towards the river. Each level has a colonnade facade, and it is only as you approach it that you appreciate its monumental scale.

Bust of the goddess Hathor at the Temple of Hatshepsut

A wide ramp, once lined with sphinxes and obelisks, on the Lower Terrace (now closed to the public) leads to a large courtyard at Middle Terrace level. A smaller ramp leads to the Upper Terrace. Behind the colonnades on the **Middle Terrace**, to the left of the ramp, carved scenes depict a trade mission bringing myrrh and incense from Egypt's neighbour Punt, present-day Somalia. A small temple dedicated to Hathor, to the left of the colonnade, has columns representing her with a cow's head, symbol of fertility. To the right, wall carvings relate scenes from the life of Queen Hatshepsut, including her divine birth: her mother is shown being attended by

Anubis, god of of the dead, known as 'the divine embalmer'

Heket, the frog-headed midwife god, watched over by Amun himself. A small temple is dedicated to the jackel-headed Anubis, god of the dead and of mummification.

If numerous carvings of Hatshepsut at the temple have been destroyed, it is because Tuthmosis III decided to remove all traces of her existence at Luxor and Karnak, when he became pharaoh after her death. But this does not spoil the formidable architectural achievement of the temple itself.

The Valley of the Kings

The **Valley of the Kings** lies out of sight across the hill behind Hatshepsut's Temple. Unlike their predecessors, the pharaohs of the New Kingdom preferred discreet tombs to monumental pyramids. As the road leads towards the valley, look for a house on the left surrounded by trees. This was the field base for Howard Carter during the long years of research that resulted in the discovery of Tutankhamun's tomb. A ticket for the Valley of the Kings includes a visit to three tombs – to visit more you must buy additional tickets. In all, more than 60 tombs have been discovered in the valley, dating from *c.*1490–

1100BC, but most are closed to the public. The most remarkable are described below.

The **Tomb of Tutankhamun** (No. 62) is certainly the best known, but the interior is disappointing. The king died very young, and artisans had only just begun to dig the chambers. His tomb is therefore small and sparsely decorated. The discovery in 1922 of the undisturbed tomb with its vast treasure trove intact is what continues to draw visitors. Also, Tutankhamun's mummy is the only one still to be found in situ – many others are on display in the Egyptian Museum in Cairo *(see page 27)*. There is an extra fee to enter the tomb.

Other tombs in the Valley of the Kings are much more instructive about Egyptian life, death and the afterlife. They are also considerably larger and more brilliantly decorated.

The **Tomb of Ramesses VI** (No. 9) reopened in 2000 after major renovations. The long tomb shaft is decorated with

Sarcophagus of Tutankhamun, discovered by Howard Carter

superb frescoes illustrating chapters of the Book of the Dead – the 'manual' of rituals to be performed in order to reach the afterlife.

The **Tomb of Seti I** (No. 17), *c.*1279BC, one of the largest and most finely decorated in the valley, is closed indefinitely. Five connecting corridors, two pits and four pillared rooms eventually lead to its burial chamber. The king pays his respects to the deities, including Ra and Kephri, as he makes his symbolic journey.

Frescoes decorating the walls of the Tomb of Ramesses VI

Exquisite frescoes in the **Tomb of Ramesses III** (No. 11) depict scenes of boats sailing on the Nile, weapons of war including spears and shields, and two harpists singing the praises of Ramesses before the deities – hence the temple's alternative name, 'Temple of the Harpists'.

It is thanks to **Ramesses IV** that many of the mummies have survived. He had them re-embalmed after tomb robbers desecrated their places of rest to steal the treasures, and devised a secret hiding place for them in a valley behind the Temple of Hatshepsut. His tomb is decorated with bas-reliefs protected by glass screens.

A splendid pink granite sarcophagus has pride of place in the **Tomb of Horemheb** (No. 57) and it's worth the walk down a long steep corridor to reach it. But the deepest in the valley (90 steps down) is the **Tomb of Amenemhet II** (No. 35). Several mummies were found here, leading to a much-improved understanding of the genealogy of the dynasties.

One of the most remote tombs, in the far west of the valley, is that of **Tuthmosis III** (No. 34), the famous son-in-law of Queen Hatshepsut. A rickety flight of steps links with the tomb entrance before you make your way down inside to the ornate burial chamber. The walls of the passage are decorated with images of more than 700 deities and the burial cham-

The Pantheon of Egyptian Gods

The religion of Ancient Egypt is characterised by the great profusion and confusion of its divinities, the country being divided between local and regional gods. The gods of one region could have different attributes in another, and the principal deities had several roles. Listed below are the most popular gods.

Ra, or **Re:** primal creator deity, controller of the universe, his symbols were the sun or obelisk. From the 5th Dynasty, human beings claimed from him a divine right to rule. Later, Amun or Amon was identified with Ra and usually depicted in human form with a ram's head.

Osiris: god of the underworld and of resurrection, depicted as a mummified pharaoh with a false beard and carrying the royal crook and flail.

Isis: goddess of fertility and motherhood, normally represented in human form wearing a crown of cow horns. Sister-wife of Osiris.

Horus: falcon-headed sun god and king of the Earth, who took human form in the ruling pharaoh. Son of Osiris.

Hathor: goddess of love and beauty; patron of women and marriage. Depicted as a cow or a woman with cow's horns. Consort of Horus.

Anubis: god of the dead, depicted with a jackal's head. Known as 'the divine embalmer' as he oversaw the mummification process.

Nut: sky goddess who swallowed the sun every evening and gave birth to it every morning.

Khnum: ram-headed god of creation; protector of the Nile source.

Thot: god of wisdom and knowledge; depicted as an ibis.

Ptah: protector of artisans; represented as a mummified man.

ber contains a finely carved red sandstone sarcophagus. Above the entrance is a royal cartouche, or hieroglyphic nameplate. Note the minimalism of the frescoes and the virtual absence of colour. Tuthmosis chose the location of his tomb well for it was not totally robbed in antiquity. Numerous artefacts found in the antechambers are now on show in the Egyptian Museum in Cairo.

Many Egyptians retain traditional dress

OTHER ATTRACTIONS IN THE NILE VALLEY

In the 1990s, several violent terrorist attacks forced the Egyptian authorities to take special security measures to assure the protection of tourists. The measures apply especially at the temples of Dendarah, Esna, Edfou, Kom Ombo and Aswan. All foreign visitors must now be accompanied by a military escort. A system of convoys at fixed times has been organised to this effect. Independent travellers should seek advice from the tourist office.

North of Luxor

Some 60km (43 miles) north of Luxor, the site of **Dendarah** ◄ (open daily 7am–5pm, 6pm in summer) is known for its temple dedicated to the cow-goddess Hathor, goddess of love. Begun in the Ptolemaic era, c.125BC, it was a major centre of female deity worship in Upper Egypt and the great Cleopatra came here to worship the goddesses. She, in turn, was adored by her subjects as a living goddess. A unique bas-relief of the queen can be seen on the rear facade of the temple, the only representation from her lifetime to have been identified.

The Romans completed the temple in AD60, and this explains the cartouches of Roman emperors on the walls. The ceilings at Dendarah illustrate the goddess Nut on her journey across the sky and are superb, although they have been blackened by the fires of Coptic Christians and Arabs who used the temple to live in. The Copts also defaced many figures of the gods. Unless you suffer from claustrophobia, don't fail to go down to the crypt, where the engravings are impeccably preserved. The roof is also accessible and offers a superb view of the whole site, the desert and the Nile valley beyond.

The hypostyle hall at the Temple of Hathor, Dendarah

To the north of Dendarah, 150km (93 miles) from Luxor, the ancient city of **Abydos** (open daily 8am–4pm, 5pm in summer) is dedicated to Osiris, god of the underworld and resurrection. This was believed to be the place where he was buried after his brother had killed him. For many centuries it was an important shrine that Egyptians would try and visit at least once in their lifetime.

The primary place of worship was the **Temple of Seti I**, with some of the finest carvings in Egypt. Built entirely of limestone, it is an impressive sight even today, and its L-shape plan is unique. It honoured generations of rulers who had passed on into the afterlife. Although Seti commissioned the temple between 1291 and 1279BC, the colonnaded courtyards and ramps were later added by his son, Ramesses II, who usurped him and tried to obliterate his name from the temple walls. Engravings on the colonnade of the second

Illustration on the facade of the Temple of Seti I at Abydos

terrace show Ramesses being welcomed by the gods – particularly Osiris, Isis and Horus. The two hypostyle halls contain some well-preserved papyrus columns; and in the Corridor of the Kings, located in the southwest wing, there are 76 cartouches listing pharaohs throughout the ages.

South of Luxor

The Nile valley south of Luxor is home to three temple complexes. These form the major stops of a Nile cruise and are all visited by tour groups from bases at Luxor or from Aswan to the south.

Esna is 54km (33 miles) by road from Luxor. The modern Egyptian town has been built on top of the ancient site of the **Temple of Khnum** (open daily 6am–4pm, 5pm in summer), the ram-headed god of creation and protector of the source of the Nile. Only the impressive hypostyle hall remains, set 9m (30ft) below the surrounding houses. The hall, begun in the reign of the Roman Emperor Tiberius, has pleasing proportions and is decorated with bas-reliefs showing the Roman emperor dressed as a pharaoh and worshipping Khnum.

Some 50km (30 miles) further south is the **Temple of Edfu** (open daily 6am–4pm, 5pm in summer), the second-largest temple in Egypt and one of the best preserved. It is dedicated to Horus – god incarnate in the ruling pharaoh – and a huge granite statue representing him as a falcon guards the temple entrance. At 79m (260ft) wide and 36m (118ft) high, the outer pylon is majestic; it was built by the Ptolemies during a total reconstruction of the temple from 237–105BC.

Edfu was built in the classic Egyptian style and was little changed during its rebuilding. Behind the pylon is a courtyard, followed by two hypostyle halls and a sanctuary. The whole structure is surrounded by a retaining wall with a narrow corridor allowing visitors to explore the carvings on the exterior walls. You see Ptolemaic pharaohs paying homage to Horus, and their sculpted food offerings are especially impressive. The back walls of the pylon have scenes relating the annual encounters between Horus and Hathor: the goddess travelled on a sacred *barque* (slender boat) from her temple at Dendarah to be reunited with her husband at his temple. This was a time of celebration for the people of Egypt, and there were two weeks of exuberant dancing, processions and feasting. At the

Statue of the falcon-god Horus at the Temple of Edfu

heart of the sanctuary, a small granite shrine once held the sacred *barque* of Horus himself. The fight between Horus and his evil uncle Seth (who had his brother Osiris, father of Horus, killed) is recreated in images on the exterior of the temple to the southwest. This incident illustrates how much the Egyptians believed in the victory of 'good over evil' through their day-to-day conduct.

Kom Ombo's hypostyle columns are rich in colour

The **Temple of Kom Ombo**, also known as the Double Temple of Horus the Elder and Sobek (open daily 7am–4pm, 5pm in summer), is 40km (24 miles) to the north of Aswan and 60km (37 miles) south of Edfu. It is situated on a high dune overlooking the Nile, and despite being badly damaged is a beautiful sight.

Before the construction of the Aswan Dam, thousands of crocodiles lived in the Nile. The Egyptians revered their strength and patience. They therefore dedicated one part of the Kom Ombo temple to Sobek, the crocodile god, and the other to Horus the Elder, the falcon god. Bas-reliefs of Sobek and Horus the Elder flank the entrance, which leads to a small room containing three badly preserved mummified crocodiles worshipped at the site. The Ptolemaic temple is unusual in that it is perfectly symmetrical on either side of the main axis, with the western part dedicated to Horus the Elder, the eastern half to Sobek. In the forecourt there is a double altar for both gods, but each side has its own hypostyle hall, inner and outer antechambers and sanctuary.

AROUND LAKE NASSER

Building the Aswan High Dam and creating Lake Nasser meant uprooting Nubia's entire population. Many ancient treasures were also relocated and can now be viewed.

Aswan

Aswan, Egypt's southernmost town, has played an important role throughout its long history. It marked the ancient border with Nubia to the south and was the conduit for the camel caravan trade in African products such as gold, ivory and spices. The word 'aswan' actually means 'trade' or 'market' in Ancient Egyptian, signifying its pre-eminent activity. The town has a high percentage of Nubians in its population; these people, though fully integrated into Egyptian society, remain proud of their separate cultural identity.

Following the decline of the Egyptian Empire, Aswan became a backwater, far removed from the power bases at Alexandria and Cairo. It began to prosper with the development of tourism, but it was the building of the **Aswan High Dam** that gave it a real boost. Some 2,000 Soviet engineers arrived to help with the mammoth project to stem the annual floods that plagued the country, and provide hydroelectricity to power a growth in industry. Completed in 1972, the dam has achieved both objectives, but the fertility of Egyptian farmland is falling as it lacks the yearly layer of fresh nutrients brought by the flood. A visit to the dam brings home the immense engineering feat achieved and allows you to gaze out over Lake Nasser, created by the blocking of the river, which is now over 500km (310 miles) in length, spanning the border with Sudan.

For the Ancient Egyptians, Aswan was the place where the annual flood of the Nile began. They could not travel upriver because several sets of cataracts blocked their passage, and they were unaware that the waters travelled from the heartland of Africa. They worshipped the Nile as the nourisher of life and built temples here to the Nile god, Hapy, and the creator god, Knum. The town was also important for the pharaohs as it sat close to one of the largest sources of high-quality granite quarries in the country, providing stone for many of its finest temples. The huge blocks were hauled to the quaysides to be carried upriver. Today, a visit to the quarries just outside town reveals some of the secrets of how the Ancient Egyptians worked the stone. A huge **unfinished obelisk** (open daily 7am–4pm, 8am–6pm in summer) lies prone: the monument fractured along a fault line and was abandoned in 1500BC. It would have been the largest in Egypt had it been completed.

Downtown Aswan has a pleasant riverside **Corniche** where you can stroll and watch the world go by. At its southern end you will find **The Old Cataract Hotel**, harking back to the

Waiting for the rush: *feluccas* on the Nile at Aswan

days of Edwardian elegance. It has seen such illustrious guests as Winston Churchill and Agatha Christie, who wrote her thriller *Death on the Nile* while staying here. From the hotel's period terrace, the river looks magnificent, making this an ideal spot for afternoon tea or a cocktail at sunset.

On the main road to the south, only a few minutes' walk from the hotel, is the imposing **Nubia Museum** (open daily 9am–1pm and 5–9pm), inaugurated in 1997. With a research facility and library dedicated to promoting Nubian traditions such as dance and music, it also houses finds rescued from several archaeological sites that were subsequently flooded by the waters of Lake Nasser in the 1970s.

Taking a traditional *felucca* out on to the Nile is one of the pleasures on offer in Aswan. These white-sailed low-draughted craft ply their way effortlessly through the water, and it is possible to view many of the town's attractions from them.

Nubian house with hieroglyphics at the Nubia Museum

On the west bank of the Nile, in a desert landscape, is the 7th-century **Coptic Monastery of St Simeon** (open daily 8am–4pm in winter, 7am–5pm in summer), sadly in ruins. The monastery can be reached on foot or by taking a camel ride from the **Tomb of the Nobles** (open 8am–4pm in winter, 7am–5pm in summer), the Old and Middle Kingdom tombs of the Princes of Elephantine.

The Aga Khan Mausoleum

Further south, overlooking Aswan, is the **Aga Khan Mausoleum** (closed to the public), the resting place of the spiritual leader of the Ismaili Muslim sect who died in 1957.

Islands of the Nile

The two islands of the Nile offer contrasting attractions. **Kitchener Island**, to the north, was offered as a gift to the British general Lord Kitchener after his victories in the Sudan in the late 19th century. He created the exotic **Botanical Gardens**, collecting plants and seeds from around the world. They are open daily 8am–5pm, 6pm in summer.

South of Kitchener Island is **Elephantine Island**, home to the **Temple of Khnum**. To honour the ram-headed god, Egyptians created a necropolis of mummified rams at the site, covering the animals' corpses with gold leaf. Some of the ram mummies are on show in the excellent small **archaeological museum** on the site. Thanks to a Roman **Nilometer** carved in the rock nearby, a strict watch could be kept on the rise and fall of the Nile, and due warning given of the annual flood. Agricultural workers could then abandon the fields in favour

The Kiosk of Emperor Trajan contains Hathor's sacred boat

of community projects such as temple building. The island can be visited daily, 7am–5pm, 6pm in summer.

The creation of **Lake Nasser** following the building of the Aswan High Dam caused many social and political concerns, not least because several monuments were going to be submerged. It was proposed that three of the most important of these should be moved to places of safety – an ambitious and costly project that was financed by UNESCO.

The **Isis Temple of Philae** (open daily 7am–4pm, 5pm in summer) was removed stone by stone to an island 5km (3 miles) south of Aswan. Known as the 'Pearl of Egypt' as much for its beauty as its setting, it was built in the 4th century BC to honour the goddess Isis, whose cult lasted longer here than elsewhere, up until the 4th century AD. It was later converted into a Coptic church, and you can see Christian crosses carved into the lintels and door frames.

The main temple was modified over centuries, and the impressive outer pylon was built in the 2nd century BC. In front, the **Kiosk of Nectanebo** (381–362BC) contains small shrines to local gods, and there is a temple to Imhotep, architect of the Step Pyramid, who was later deified. Inside the main temple, the small birthing chamber, or *mammisi*, is decorated with bas-reliefs of Isis holding her new-born son Horus. A second pylon shows Ptolemy XIII paying homage to Isis, flanked by Osiris and Horus. The Romans continued the cult of Isis at Philae, adding their own variations. The beautiful **Kiosk of Emperor Trajan**, with ornate floral capitals supported by elegant columns, makes a striking contrast to the Egyptian temple designs.

The sound-and-light show at Philae is one of the best, and it's worth spending an extra night in Aswan to see it. The times vary, so ask at your hotel or the tourist office.

Abu Simbel

The temples of **Abu Simbel** (open 6am–5pm, until 6pm in summer) are among the greatest architectural achievements of Ancient Egypt, and among the best known. Rather than build them from stone, Ramesses II had the temples hewn into the cliffs of the Nile valley, on a site in ancient Nubia 7km (4 miles) from the border with Sudan. The construction of the Aswan High Dam in 1972 and the creation of Lake Nasser threatened to flood the temple complex, so it was decided to remove them to a similar setting where there was no risk of flooding. An artificial cliffside was created on higher ground, replicating the original in every dimension. The temple complex was then dismantled into over 1000 pieces – some weighed up to 15 tons

One of four colossi guarding the Temple of Ramesses II

Divine sun

The inner sanctum of the Ramesses II Temple was aligned so that the first rays of the sun on 21 February and 21 October would fall on the seated statues of four gods, Ptah of Memphis, Amun-Ra of Thebes, the deified Ramesses II and Ra-Herekhty, the sun-god of Heliopolis.

– transported to the new site and reassembled. The reconstruction is virtually perfect. Ramesses II built these temples in the 13th century BC, at the height of his power, imposing his authority throughout his kingdom. As well as symbolising his power, the temples were used to store gold and other precious cargos that arrived from central Africa by camel.

The facade of the **Temple of Ramesses II** (open daily 6am–5pm, 6pm in summer) is one of the most enduring images of Egypt – it is used on the front of numerous guides and brochures – but nothing can prepare you for the reality which is truly breathtaking. The four monumental colossi of Ramesses II that frame the entrance stand 20m (65ft) high and face the rising sun, to be infused with the energy of the sun god each day. The pharaoh is seated, imperturbable, wearing the double crown signifying his control over both Upper and Lower Egypt. At his feet are his family, represented as diminutive figures. Bas-reliefs carved on the pharaoh's thrones depict the Nile gods. Between the two central colossi is an alcove with a small statue to Ra-Herekhty (Ra the sun god combined with Horus) with whom Ramesses shares the temple.

This temple has no forecourt so you enter directly into the **Hypostyle Hall**. Carvings on the columns show Ramesses (in the form of Osiris) making offerings to the gods, and the walls show scenes from his military campaigns, returning in triumph with hundreds of Hittite prisoners. The north side is almost entirely devoted to the most important victory of his reign, the Battle of Qadesh, in which the young pharaoh overcame the Hittite tribe near the Syrian town of Qadesh.

Near the temple of Ramesses II is the smaller **Temple of Nefertari**, his beloved wife. She, too, is deified and in a facade of six colossi 11.5m (38ft) high, she stands at equal height to her husband – a rare honour for a consort in Egypt. However, of the six statues only two are of Nefertari, the other four are consecrated to Ramesses, maintaining his position of superiority. Within the sanctuary dedicated to Hathor is a room where Ramesses and Nefertari made offerings to the gods, as well as carvings showing the pharaoh himself worshipping his deified wife.

Most people take the regular flights from Aswan to Abu Simbel, which take around 50 minutes. For security reasons, most travellers going overland to Abu Simbel are made to travel in convoys of organised tours.

The superb colossi at the entrance to the Temple of Nefertari

THE OASES OF THE WESTERN DESERT

These isolated pockets of fertile land are a welcome contrast to the dusty capital, or the busy Nile towns. The oases thrived under the Romans, when they were important stops on the trade routes, but after the fall of the Roman Empire they slipped into decline. In 1958 President Nasser created the New Valley to resettle people from the Nile Valley to the oases, however there was never enough work to attract the masses. The towns have developed considerably since the beginning of the 21st century, and are nowadays inhabited by Berbers from North Africa and Egyptians escaping the overpopulation of the Nile Valley. With their acres of date palms, apricot and olive trees, they also a tourist attraction.

A two-hour drive from Cairo is the semi-oasis of al-Fayyum, near Lake Qarun, where King Faruq liked to hunt.

Perfect geometry: sand dunes in the Western Desert

Archaeological remains from Egyptian and Roman times lie scattered in the farmland. **Al-Bahariyyah**, the closest oasis from Cairo (330km/ 205 miles), has several small ancient sites in its lush gardens. From there a good road through the White Desert leads to **Farafrah**, the smallest of these oases. **Dakhlah** has a certain laid-back charm and several Roman temples and remains. **Khargah**, Egypt's largest oasis, has an airport but is the least picturesque.

Dates flourish in the oases

Siwah, the most fascinating oasis, near the Libyan border, is reached by a road from Marsa Matruh or by the new road from al-Bahariyyah. Alexander the Great came here to consult the oracle at the **Temple of Jupiter-Amun**. Bicycles, for rent in Siwah town, are the best way to visit the main sites. Nearby are the magnificent sand dunes of Great Sand Sea with numerous hot and cold lakes.

THE RED SEA COAST AND THE SUEZ CANAL

After pacing round the hot and impressive archaeological sites of the Nile Valley, or the noisy streets of Cairo, the Red Sea coast makes a refreshing contrast. The sea breeze and sandy beaches combine with hotels and restaurants to provide a relaxing holiday. The coast was not developed until the 1990s, but buildings now stretch all along the shoreline. The main town is **Hurghada**, whose small offshore islands offer exceptional diving. Although somewhat lacking in charm, it has its own airport and offers a number of good resort hotels and a pleasant environment in nearby Al-Gouna.

At the northern tip of the Red Sea coast, where the African continent meets the Sinai peninsula, is one of the greatest feats of modern technology, the **Suez Canal**. This man-made passage connects the Mediterranean with the Red Sea and Indian Ocean. Opened in 1869, it allowed a much quicker journey time from Europe to the Middle East, India and the Far East, and was a huge aid to the Western European powers in managing their empires. Today, tourists travel almost exclusively by plane, but the Suez Canal is still vital for cargo vessels. Watching a giant tanker travel through the passage is a unique experience: unless you're standing beside the canal you can't see the water and the vessel seems to float along on the sand.

The Suez Canal

The idea of a building a canal to link the Red Sea with the Mediterranean was an ancient one. In the 7th century BC Necho II, a pharaoh of the 26th Dynasty, put forward a project to join the Gulf of Suez to the Nile – and thence to the Mediterranean – but he was dissuaded. In 521 BC Egypt's Persian conquerors, under Darius, began work on a canal between Ismaïlia and Cairo. Despite Roman re-excavation c.AD 100, no trace of it remained under the caliphs seven centuries later.

In the 19th century, an ambitious plan for a canal cut across the narrow isthmus of Suez was promoted by the French engineer Ferdinand de Lesseps, who eventually convinced Saïd Pacha of its merits. With the backing of a commission of European countries the great project was begun in 1859. It took 10 years and 25,000 labourers to cut the 160-km (100-mile) channel from Suez to Port Saïd. Opened in 1869, and nationalised in 1956, the canal was blocked by Egypt during the Arab-Israeli war of 1967 and not reopened until 1975 by President Sadat.

SINAI

This easternmost part of Egypt is sparsely populated, and was the object of discord between Egypt and Israel in the 1950s and 1960s. Occupied by Israel for several years, it was returned to Egypt in 1979.

Sinai is a magnificent wild land pointing south into the Red Sea. The desert terrain of the north rises in the south to granite peaks that contrast with the azure blue of the sea. Ancient seismic activity formed the mountain range, which was then sculpted by wind and frost into bizarre shapes. Very lit-

Strange sculpture: Sinai heights

tle flourishes here – an acacia tree here and there, the odd desert fox on the look-out or a family of wild camels. Sinai has long been the domain of the Bedouin, nomadic tribes crossing the deserts with their flocks of sheep and camels.

Ancient Egyptians valued Sinai as a source of turquoise, but its real glory comes from Gebel Musa, the mount where, according to tradition, Moses received the Ten Commandments from God, the basis of the world's three monotheistic religions.

Sinai remained apart from the ravages of the modern world until the the development of underwater diving. Armed with oxygen cylinders, the world's divers have discovered the astonishing wealth of coral, fish and marine life to be found in Sinai's exceptionally clear coastal waters.

During the 1950s and 1960s **Sharm al-Shaykh**, situated on the southern tip of the Sinai, became a divers' paradise. The village has since seen a multitude of hotels, restaurants, bars and shops spread along the seafront. **Na'ama Bay**, some 5km (3 miles) further north, has sandy beaches, modern hotels and tourist infrastructure. The terrorist bombings here on 23 July 2005 have had an inevitable impact on tourism. Security has been increased and a protective fence built around the resort.

In the 1980s, the Egyptian government responded to the rise in tourism here by creating **Ras Muhammad National Park** (open daily 9am–5pm) to protect the waters and their inhabitants. Considered one of the premier diving sites in the world, it encompasses several marine ecosystems and is home to more than 1,000 species of fish, marine animals and corals. It is possible to explore the deeps with full diving equipment or simply snorkel here. Those who don't want to get wet can glimpse this watery world on a glass-bottom boat or submarine tour. Ras Muhammad also protects the shoreline environment here, including rare mangrove forests with abundant bird life.

Tourist development in the Sinai is mainly concentrated along the east coast where it meets the waters of the Gulf of Aqaba, though there can be many miles between resorts. Both **Dahab** and **Nuweiba** are thriving resorts but fortunately remain less developed than Sharm al-Shaykh. They are both well equipped for diving, windsurfing and other watersports. At the very northern tip of the Sinai is the resort of **Taba**, with several large hotels, marking the Egyptian-Israeli border.

Underwater exploration

Mount Sinai

A point of pilgrimage for generations, **Mount Sinai** was endowed with a Christian place of worship as early as AD527, when Emperor Justinian built a small orthodox monastery there. Situated in the lea of the mountain surrounded by sheer rock faces, it was also built to protect the Sinai pass against invasion. The church was constructed on the traditional spot where Moses confronted the Burning Bush. The Christian community subsequently fortified the complex with high surrounding walls.

Monastery of St Catherine

Inside the **Monastery of St Catherine** (open daily except Fri and Sun 9.30–11.45am) the complex, still home to a community of Greek Orthodox monks, is centred on St Catherine's Church, dating from 552. The saint's remains were discovered nearby on Mount St Catherine around 300 years later. The church houses some of the monastery's treasures donated by wealthy benefactors.

St Catherine's has long been a wealthy and influential monastery, founding school throughout the Orthodox world. The richly decorated iconostasis has superb icons painted by Jeremias of Crete in 1612, but the 6th-century mosaics on the ceiling of the apse and the library of ancient manuscripts are the most impressive features of the church. St Catherine's skull lies within an 18th-century marble tomb.

WHAT TO DO

In addition to its wonderful archaeological sites along the Nile, Egypt offers an array of cultural and sporting activities worthy of interest.

ENTERTAINMENT

From fiction to films, Egypt is at the hub of popular culture in the Arab world. There is also a wealth of live entertainment of all kinds. Check details of any festivals or events *(see page 97)* that may concide with your visits.

Sound-and-Light Shows

All the most impressive ancient sites in Egypt have a sound-and-light show – something that should add an extra dimension to your experience of ancient Egyptian culture. At Giza there is a nightly show in English at the pyramids. At Luxor the show is held at Karnak Temple. Unusually for a show of this sort, spectators wander among the obelisks and columns, as the story unfolds, then remain seated by the sacred lake for the rest of the show. At Aswan the sound-and-light show takes place at Philae Temple, some 20 minutes from the town. For information on all sound-and-light shows, tel: 02-3863469, <www.sound-light.egypt.com>. Remember to take warm clothing during the winter months, as the evenings can be chilly.

Folkloric Events

Many Beduin of the Sinai have abandoned their wandering ways in favour of a more settled life, but they still prefer to live in tents rather than houses and maintain their traditional

Guiding a *felucca* along the Nile

customs. Some Beduin families have opened up their homes to visitors, and it is possible to share an evening meal with them and discover more about their culture.

In Upper Egypt, Nubian floorshows have a special atmosphere. They are performed in all the large hotels, bringing traditional music and dancing into the 21st century. Most large hotels also put on floorshows featuring music and belly-dancing; spectators invariably end up participating.

The at-Tannoura Egyptian Heritage Dance Troupe does a 90-minute performance of traditional Sufi dancing (similar to that of the Whirling Dervishes). Free performances are held at Cairo's al-Ghuri Mausoleum (al-Azhar Street, at the foot of the pedestrian bridge) on Wed and Sat at 6.30pm. The band Mazaher performs traditional Egyptian and *zar* (exorcism) music at Makan (1 Darih Saad Street, al-Mounira) on Wed at 9pm.

Nightlife

Belly-dancing. Not just a tourist show, it's also popular with Egyptians, and you can take in a serious and perhaps more earthy show at several clubs around the capital.

Casinos. There are more than a dozen casinos in Cairo, mostly in the major hotels, with their rich habitués. Egyptian nationals are not allowed to gamble, so the clientele is exclusively foreign. You must be aged over 21 and show some form of ID.

Clubs. Found in the major international hotels, these are popular with Egyptians and visitors alike.

Opera. The Cairo Opera House (tel: 02 739 8144, <www.operahouse.gov.eg>) stages international opera and ballet, and performances by the Cairo Opera and Cairo Symphony Orchestra. Programmes are available at the information window or online. Men have to wear jacket and tie in the Main Hall.

SPORTS AND OUTDOOR ACTIVITIES

For snorkelling and diving, the coral peninsula at the tip of Sinai is hard to beat. If you want a change from Egypt's beach-based options, you can always take off into the desert.

Watersports

Beaches. Superb beaches with fine sand line the Red Sea, the west coast and the southern tip of the Sinai Peninsula as well as the Mediterranean. In general, the Red Sea and Sinai attract foreign tourists, while the Mediterranean coastal resorts cater mostly to Egyptians. Sharm al-Shaykh and Hurghada are the largest resorts, with numerous hotels, restaurants and watersport facilities. Dahab and Nuweiba on the west coast of Sinai are smaller, with a hardened diving or windsurfing crowd. Temperatures rarely go below 20°C (70°F).

Sublime turquoise waters near Hurghada, on the Red Sea

Over 90 percent of Egypt is desert – ideal for a sand safari

Snorkelling and diving. Egypt offers great opportunities for both diving and snorkelling – the southern tip of the Sinai peninsula is one of the world's prime dive sites. Ras Muhammad National Park has more than 1,000 species of fish and 150 types of coral, and there is diving for all abilities. The reefs run all the way up the eastern coast of the Sinai peninsula, punctuated by the resorts of Dahab, Nuweiba and Sharm al-Shaykh. Across a small strait from Ras Muhammad National Park is Hurghada, with fantastic sea and coral life.

Learning to dive in Egypt is easy thanks to the numerous dive centres that offer training at all levels. All centres are affiliated with a certifying body such as PADI (Professional Association of Diving Instructors). The basic qualification takes five days to complete, and with it you can dive with an instructor to a depth of 18m (60ft) in any of Egypt's many dive sites. Most training centres also offer an introductory diving session. This involves a half-day of theory and swimming pool work, to learn the basic techniques before signing up for a course. Many large hotels offer this 'taster' to their guests. Emperor Divers (<www.emperordivers.com>), a long-established firm, has offices at Hurghadah, Na'ama Bay and Nuweiba.

If you don't want to explore the depths then you can snorkel in shallow offshore waters along the Red Sea and Sinai coasts to see excellent tropical marine life. Snorkelling equipment is on sale at the resorts.

You can also take a ride in a glass-bottomed boat or the Sindbad submarine (tel: 065 344 4688, <www.sindbad-group.com>) to see the fascinating underwater environment.

Fishing. All the coastal resorts have marinas where you can rent boats to go fishing for a morning or a day. Weekly fishing safaris on Lake Nasser are offered by African Angler (<www.african-angler.co.uk>, tel: 097 230 9748) and Lake Nasser Adventure (<www.lakenasseradventure.com>, tel: 012 240 5897).

Excursions and Rides

Safaris and desert excursions. Over 90 percent of Egypt's land is desert, and it is becoming increasingly popular as a perfect antidote to stressed urban life. You can take safaris lasting from one to three days on camel, or by four-wheel-drive (where all supplies are included), or simply head off on quad bikes for an afternoon of fun in the sand dunes.

Longer safaris in the Western Desert are available from Peter Gaballa at Egypt Off Road (<www.egyptoffroad.com>, tel: 010 147 5462), Khalifa Expedition (tel: 02-8473261, <www.khalifaexp.com>) and Amr Shannon (tel: 02-5196894, email: <ashannon@internetegypt.com>). Most hotels in Sinai and on the Red Sea can organise shorter trips in the desert.

Camel rides and horseback riding. Camel rides and treks can be taken around the pyramids, at Luxor and Aswan, at every resort in Sinai and on the Red Sea coast. Horseback riding is also offered in Sinai, the Red Sea, Cairo and Luxor.

Other sports. The Gazirah Sports Club, on Zamalek Island, Cairo, offers temporary membership, which allows access to facilities including tennis and squash courts, handball courts and swimming pools. The Oberoi Mena House Hotel operates an 18-hole golf club near the pyramids at Giza; you don't have to be a guest to enjoy the facilities.

SHOPPING

There's something for all budgets in Egypt and the souvenir industry is flourishing. The skills of carvers, weavers and painters have been passed down through the generations and you can spend hours admiring their work. However, Egyptian shopkeepers are tenacious: you'll need a strong will and a sense of humour to shrug off their sales pitch. If you take a guide or interpreter with you, it is customary for them to receive a percentage on every purchase you make.

Most reputable vendors can arrange to ship abroad any items that are too large or too fragile to carry home.

An Egyptian weaver in a souk

Where to Shop

Bazaars. Khan al-Khalili and the surrounding area in Cairo is one of the oldest bazaars in the Muslim world. A veritable treasure trove of shopping opportunities, the labyrinth of narrow alleys is divided into 'quarters', each with its own speciality. The tent-making

This stall in the Khan specialises in covers for pouffes

bazaar outside Bab Zuwaylah, where large ceremonial tents are fashioned by hand from brightly dyed Egyptian cotton, is particularly interesting. The Khan, as it is known locally, is not just a tourist bazaar. The Egyptians shop here too, and it offers a chance to mingle with them to find artefacts from around the country. There is a smaller but no less atmospheric bazaar at Luxor. At Aswan the main shopping street runs parallel to the river. Its souk sells Egyptian, Nubian and African handicrafts.

Archaeological sites. Mini-tourist markets have sprung up around most of the major archaeological sites. They all sell much the same items as the larger bazaars and souks, but prices are likely to be higher. The quality of goods varies from one stall to another, and a common ploy is to sell inferior stone painted to look like marble or alabaster, so be wary of bargains. Prices drop at the end of the day, after the tour groups leave, especially out of season.

Hieroglyphic cartouches
are popular items of jewellery

What to Buy

Alabaster and marble.
Carving skills have been passed down through the centuries, notably in villages near the Valley of the Kings and around the marble quarries at Aswan. From beautiful copies of ancient pieces to inexpensive souvenirs, you will be spoilt for choice. Small items, such as scarab beetles – considered lucky in Egypt – are sold in shops, but also by young children and street hawkers around the archaeological sites.

Copper and brass. These metals have long been used for practical items such as water carriers, samovars or cooking pots, and they make excellent souvenirs. Older pieces have the patina of age, whereas new pieces – usually made on site – are bright and shiny. Trays can be found in all sizes and those with a wooden stand make good portable tables.

Jewellery. Given the amount of gold buried in Egyptian tombs, it's not surprising that gold is a good buy. Precious metals are sold by weight, with very little added to the price for workmanship. Precious stones and semi-precious stones including topaz, lapis lazuli and aquamarine, can be bought loose or set in rings, necklaces, bracelets or brooches.

Copies of ancient hieroglyphic cartouches also make very popular souvenirs – a jeweller can have your name made up into a cartouche of Egyptian script in just a couple of hours.

Cotton and woollen goods. Egyptian cotton, with its long fibres, is arguably the finest in the world. The thousands of hectares under cultivation in the Nile Delta are one of the country's most lucrative export earners, though it is hard to find fine quality Egyptian cotton in Egypt itself. Almost everywhere you go you'll come across cotton *gallabiyas* – the long dress-like garments worn by men and women – and a variety of T-shirts featuring camels and pyramids. Other natural fibres are made into beautiful scarves, shawls and blankets. Those made of sheep's wool are the most common, followed by camel-hair varieties and silk or silk-blended items.

Bargaining

Bargaining is part of Egyptian folklore. It's a social act, a discussion between two people – buyer and seller.

Bargaining requires humour and patience. It is not a battle, more a form of verbal gymnastics to achieve a win-win outcome. Cups of tea or coffee traditionally help things along, although nowadays you might be offered a cola instead. Accepting a cup of tea means you are serious about buying; it's the first step in the negotiation.

The starting price is usually high. Reject it, but don't insult the vendor with a ludicrously low counter-offer. The final price will be around 30–50 percent less than the starting price. Do a quick calculation; if you don't think you will reach agreement, refuse politely but firmly with a handshake and a smile. By contrast, if the starting price seems a reasonable basis, make a lower offer than the price you have in mind to pay. Gradually, through words and gestures, you will reach agreement on a mutually acceptable price. It is a good idea to agree on a strategy with a companion beforehand. Feigned nonchalance by your friend can work in your favour.

Once the deal is finally sealed you will come away not only with a beautiful object but also the memory of a special interaction.

Woodwork. Muslim tradition frowns on the use of precious metals in its religious buildings, so artisans working more basic raw materials have always been held in high regard in the Arab world. Egypt – particularly Cairo – is renowned for its wood carvers, who still produce beautiful hand-worked pieces in small workshops in the old part of the city. Whether it be a tiny box or a large coffee table, the detail is always exquisite.

The finest, most authentic work is *mashrabiya*, the lattice screens that covered Ottoman windows allowing women to watch the world go by without being seen. These are now re-produced in miniature for picture frames or as screens. More easily transported are boxed chess and backgammon sets made from wood inlaid with mother of pearl or ivory. Don't worry about the risk to endangered animal species: most Egyptian ivory is camel or donkey bone, not elephant tusk.

Papyrus. The leaves of the papyrus, a particular type of reed, were dried and used by Ancient Egyptians as a form of paper. The art of papyrus-making was lost, but it was reintroduced in the 1970s using native plants. Today, almost every souvenir shop sells inexpensive papyrus painted with Egyptian scenes.

Most authentic are those sold at Dr Ragab's Papyrus Institute on Shari an-Nil in Dokki, Cairo (tel: 02-3367212, <www.papyrusin stitute.com>) as the papyrus is grown, processed and hand-painted on site.

Painted papyrus

Spices. There are plenty of spices for sale in Egyptian souks, but stick to those that Egyptians use on a daily

Display of colourful, pungent spices at the souk in Aswan

basis: cumin *(kamum)*, black pepper *(filfil)*, koreander *(kosbara)*, chilli *(shatta)*, fenugreek *(hilba)* and cinnamon *(irfa)*. Look out, particularly in Aswan, for the dried hibiscus flowers *(karkadeh)*, which make a delicious hot or cold drink. Other spices are used in traditional medicine. Avoid buying saffron, which is expensive and of very bad quality in Egypt.

Perfume. The elite of Ancient Egypt had a taste for luxury, and incense, aromatic oils and perfumes made from petals were part of their daily life. Perfumes are still popular to this day, and in the bazaars you will find perfume sellers surrounded by hundreds of glass bottles containing different oils for blending. You can either ask for your favourite scent to be recreated for you, or choose a blend recommended for your skin type. But beware, as the finest natural oils are expensive and rare; most of what is for sale is made from chemicals or bad-quality concoctions.

CHILDREN

Egyptians adore children, and are very sweet with them. Most children love Egypt and are fascinated by the stories and the sights. The secret is not to do too much in a day, especially in the heat, and to alternate sightseeing with other fun activities. Listed below are a few children-friendly activities.

• Climb inside the Great Pyramid of Giza, or in the deeper tombs in the Valley of the Kings, and they will feel like Indiana Jones or Tintin themselves.

Few kids can resist a camel ride

• Visit Giza's Pharaonic Village (tel: 02-5718675; <www.touregypt.net/village/history.htm>) and let children discover (rather than simply imagine) Ancient Egyptian life.

• Take a *felucca* trip on the Nile or a glass-bottomed boat along the Red Sea and Sinai coasts (*see page 89*).

• Go horse or camel riding near the Pyramids in Cairo, on the West Bank in Luxor or at the resorts on the Red Sea or Sinai.

• Don't miss the Mummy Room at the Egyptian Museum in Cairo. Most children love the rather gory-looking pharaohs and find the process of mummification fascinating.

• Ride in a horse-drawn carriage along the corniche next to the Nile at Luxor or Aswan.

• Book a hotel with a pool, so that you can have a relaxing swim after a day spent sightseeing.

Festivals and Events

Most Muslim festivals are determined by the Islamic calendar, based on the lunar cycle. As lunar months are shorter than our solar months, the dates vary from year to year. The calendar starts at the Higra in AD 622, the year the Prophet Muhammad left Mecca for Medina.

Ramadan The main event in the Islamic calendar is Ramadan, the ninth month, when all Muslims fast between sunrise and sunset. A cannon shot announces the time for breaking the fast, and the night-long party begins. *Aïd el-Fitr* marks Ramadan's end, with celebrations, family visits and gifts.

Aïd al-Adha (or *Aïd al-Kabir*) marks the time of the *hajj*, the pilgrimage to Mecca. The feast lasts three days, and those families who can afford it slaughter a sheep to commemorate the sacrifice of Abraham.

Mouled an-Nabi celebrates the Prophet Mohammed's birthday, with street parties and Sufi gatherings near the main mosques.

Other festivals and events include:

7 January Coptic Christmas.

19 January Epiphany.

February Luxor Marathon where competitors race around the ancient sights (see <www.egyptianmarathon.com>).
Nitaq Festival, a contemporary arts festival in downtown Cairo.

April–May Coptic Easter.
Sham an-Nessim Spring Festival, held the Monday after Coptic Easter. For this big festival – the name means 'sniffing the breeze' – Egyptians, Muslims and Christians all take part in festivities directly descended from Ancient Egypt to celebrate the resurrection of Osiris and the return of spring. Families traditionally have a picnic of *fasikh*, dried fish with eggs and onions.

25 April Sinai Liberation Day.

1 May Labour Day.

23 July Revolution Day, commemorating the 1952 revolution.

September Experimental Theatre Festival in Cairo.

October Pharaoh's Rally for 4x4s and motorbikes through the desert.

December Cairo International Film Festival.

EATING OUT

In a country with such a long history, it is fascinating to think that some of the staples of Egyptian food enjoyed by contemporary Egyptians were already popular at the time of the pharaohs. Just as depicted in ancient frescoes, the basic ingredients of Egyptian cuisine are still the same: the fish of the Mediterranean, the Red Sea and the Nile, the rice, corn and vegetables grown in the Nile Valley, the sheep and goats of the delta, the pigeons and ducks reared by rural families.

Sun-ripened: Egypt has fruit and vegetables in abundance

Egyptian cuisine essentially consists of simple but delicious peasant dishes, using vegetables from the local marketplace. Over the centuries, as Egypt was continuously under foreign occupation, Roman, Persian, Arab, Ottoman and French dishes all found their way into the local cuisine. More recently European and American influences have become more noticeable, and in the trendy restaurants of Cairo 'global fusion' is now on the menu. Similarly, most of the larger hotels in the main tourist towns have several international restaurants catering for visitors as well as the more adventurous, wealthy Egyptians.

When to Eat

Most smaller hotels serve Continental-style breakfasts, while the larger hotels lay on superb buffets with fruit, cereals, charcuterie and hot dishes. Egyptians have '*fuul*' (pronounced 'fool') for breakfast, which is a stew of fava beans *(see page 100)*, often eaten with pitta. *Fuul* carts can be seen on every street corner in the early

A copious Egyptian breakfast

morning. For the Egyptians, lunch is the main meal of the day, eaten between 1pm and 3pm. Dinner, a lighter meal, is served up to 10pm. However, most restaurants are adapted to foreign tourists and follow Western rhythms. During the month of Ramadan, when Muslims fast during the hours of daylight, special arrangements are made for both the meal to break the fast *(iftar)* and the meal to commence the fast *(sohour)*. Most international hotel restaurants in big towns continue to serve foreigners during the day, but you are unlikely to find a resturant open in small provincial towns.

EGYPTIAN CUISINE

The development of tourism saw Egyptian cuisine take a back seat to international fare. Now restaurateurs have regained confidence and serve excellent national specialities.

Appetisers

The meal often starts with a shared plate of *mezze*, an assortment of local cheeses, salads, stuffed vine leaves, *kofta* (fried meatballs with spices and coriander), *makhallal* (pickled vegetables), *tabouleh* (crushed bulgar wheat mixed with parsley, mint, finely chopped tomatoes and onions), *tahina* (sesame seed purée), *hummus* (chickpea purée) and *baba ganoug* (*tahina* with puréed aubergine, garlic and lemon juice). These last three are scooped up with fresh warm pitta (unleavened bread) cooked in a wood-fired oven.

Soup is another popular choice. Lentil soup *(shorbet ads)* is found all over Egypt and fish soup is a speciality along the coast. A favourite among Egyptians and popular since the time of the pharaohs, *meloukhia* is a broth made from Jew's Mallow (not unlike spinach), seasoned with garlic, pepper and coriander, and served with rice and roast chicken or rabbit – more a main course than a starter.

Nuts and dried fruits enliven national dishes

A traditional dish served at any meal and a favourite to break the Ramadan fast is *fuul*, a thick and spicy bean stew cooked for six hours or so, accompanied by *taamia*, deep-fried fava bean paste flavoured with vegetables, spices and parsley.

Main Dishes

Meat. Although meat has long been a luxury ingredient for ordinary Egyptians, they have developed some delicious ways of serving it. On feast days whole goats or sheep are cooked for the entire neighbourhood, either on an open charcoal grill or in a covered wood-fired oven. Lamb and goat meat is often marinated beforehand in fresh herbs and spices that enhance the meaty flavour.

Ever-popular, *kebabs* are grilled skewered chunks of meat; *kofta* is grilled minced lamb cooked on a skewer; and *shwarma* is lamb roasted on a vertical spit, thinly sliced and served with salad and pitta bread. Grilled or barbecued chicken is also popular; less common are

Traditional hand-made *pittas*

goose or duck. Many farmers rear pigeons *(hamam)* and quail. Both are normally stuffed with fenugreek and served on a bed of rice.

Fish and seafood. There's plenty of Mediterranean and Red Sea fish – notably sea bream, red and grey mullet and sea bass – but prices are higher than for meat dishes. Large, succulent Alexandrian shrimp are delicious, as are spiny lobster from the Red Sea, squid and cuttlefish. Few fish come from the Nile, though freshwater tilapia from Lake Nasser is usually excellent. A delicacy that is now quite rare is *betarekh*, dried salted cod roe served on bread soaked in olive oil. The Ancient Egyptians claimed that it had aphrodisiac powers.

Side Dishes and Accompaniments

Rice is generally served with main courses, though you can have fries. As most food in Egypt is served warm rather than hot (hot food is said to be bad for the digestion), those expecting crisp fries will be disappointed. Seasonal salads are available, including plates of sliced beetroot or cucumber.

Desserts

Most Egyptian desserts are very rich and sweet. Try *om-ali* (bread pudding baked with milk, coconut, raisins and nuts), divine when it's well prepared; or treat yourself to one of the sweet pastries introduced during Ottoman rule. *Baklava*, butter-soaked flaky pastry interspersed with nuts and honey, is the most famous. *Konafa*, made from shredded filo pastry filled with pistachios or thick cream, is marginally less sweet, and *basbousa*, a semolina cake drenched in syrup with nuts, is another favourite.

Depending on the season, you'll also be offered bananas, oranges, figs, melons, pomegranates or guavas to finish off your meal. Dates come in several varieties and are delicious

Sweet and elaborate cakes and pastries are typical

when fresh – quite different from the dried dates sold in the West. Fresh or dried, they are on sale in all the markets and are worth buying to stave off hunger pangs when sightseeing.

International Cuisine

In Cairo and the main tourist towns there are numerous restaurants serving Western-style food, and most large hotels have a choice of restaurants. Along the Red Sea and Sinai coasts, you'll find a plethora of pizza parlours, Bierkellers and Chinese restaurants. Many Egyptian restaurants now offer hamburgers in addition to other grilled meats.

DRINKS

Although Egypt is an Islamic country and many Egyptians do not drink alcohol, the sale of alcoholic drinks is legal. In fact, vines have been cultivated in the Nile delta since time immemorial. Among the local wines, Omar Khayyam and Obélisque Rouge are soft, fairly dry reds. White wines, such as Cru des Ptolemées or Blanc d'Alexandrie, are often better than the reds but may not be served sufficiently chilled. The new more upmarket Grand de Marquise has by far the best wines, both red and white. Rubis d'Egypte and Obélisque Rosetta are good rosés to be drunk on their own or with food. Imported wines are found in international hotels and the better restaurants, with a high mark-up. Wine lists may be limited during Ramadan.

If you would like something a little stronger than wine ask for *zibib*, an Egyptian aniseed-flavoured spirit similar to Greek *ouzo*, which is made from distilling grape skins; or try a strong and

> ### Alcohol
>
> Out of respect for Islamic tradition, avoid drinking alcohol in public, except at hotels and restaurants catering to tourists.

slightly sweeter date brandy. International spirits such as gin, whisky and cognac are imported, as are some beers. The local Stella beer has been bottled in Cairo for more than 100 years and is good when served cold. Even better is a cold Saqqara beer, brewed in al-Gouna on the Red Sea coast.

Tea *(shay)* is ubiquitous in Egypt – it is served throughout the day, offered at bazaars when you shop, and drunk by Egyptian men playing backgammon at cafés. Traditionally it is served strong with lots of sugar and milk, though often a sprig of mint will be added if there is no milk. Many cafés also serve herbal teas such as *helba* (fenugreek), *yansoon* (anis) and *sahlab* (arrowroot). *Karkadeh*, a drink made from dried hibiscus petals, can be served chilled –

A Smoker's Paradise

In Egyptian cafés you frequently see men – and occasionally women nowadays – smoking a *sheesha*. This water pipe, also known as a *hookah*, cools, sweetens and lightens the taste of the burning tobacco leaves and makes a soothing gurgle.

The *sheesha* uses essentially two types of tobacco. By far the most popular is *maassil*, a sticky blend of chopped leaf fermented with molasses, which gives the smoke a sweet taste. The *maassil* is pressed into small clay bowls which are fitted into the *sheesha* and lit with charcoal. *Toumbak* is loose dry tobacco wrapped into a cone with a whole leaf, and is a lot rougher to smoke.

Traditionally men smoke the *sheesha*, but in the cities it very fashionable for women to smoke as well. The trendy cafés and restaurants now offer a range of flavoured tobaccos, including mint, apple, date, strawberry and even cappuccino, and customers often smoke while eating *mezzeh* and drinking. More and more cafés provide disposable plastic mouthpieces to fit on the end of the *sheesha*. In the old days hashish was smoked in some cafés, but this has not been legal for a long time.

refreshing in summer – or hot as a tea, but always very sweet. It is often served at the start of the meal, especially during Ramadan, and is said to aid digestion.

The strong coffee introduced by the Ottoman Turks remains a favourite with Egyptians, who generally enjoy it *ziyada*, with lots of sugar. You may prefer it *mazbut* (medium) or *saadeh* (without sugar). If you want just a pinch of sugar, ask for a *qahwa ar-riha*.

Tap water in Egypt should be avoided in favour of bottled water. Brands include Baraka, Siwa, Safi or Delta. Alternatively, fresh fruit juices of orange, pomegranate, carrot, mango and guava are also widely available.

Veteran smokers of the *sheesha* in an Egyptian café

To Help You Order...

bread	**aysh**	potatoes	**batatis**
butter	**zibda**	rice	**roz**
chicken	**firakh**	soup	**shorba**
chickpeas	**hommos**	sugar	**sokkar**
coffee	**ahwa/qahwa**	tea	**shay**
fava stew	**fuul**	wine	**nabeet**
dates	**balagh**	boiled	**maslook**
fish	**samak**	fried	**makhli**
meat	**lahma**	grilled	**mashwi**

HANDY TRAVEL TIPS

An A–Z Summary of Practical Information

A

ACCOMMODATION

Egypt has excellent hotels in the higher star brackets but less choice in the mid-range categories. Many three- to five-star hotels are contracted to tour groups, so accommodation for independent travellers can be hard to find, especially from December–April in Cairo and the Nile Valley, and June–August in Alexandria and coastal regions.

Hotels' rates for anyone arriving on spec are high. If possible, pre-book your accommodation before you leave home and take confirmation of your bookings to avoid problems at check-in. Prices are usually in US dollars. Three- to five-star hotels accept payment in foreign currency or by credit card. *See also hotel listings on pages 128–35.*

AIRPORTS

Egypt's main airport is situated 20km (12 miles) northwest of Cairo's town centre. It has two terminals: Terminal 2 is for all American and Western European airlines, and Terminal 1 which handles all other flights. Both terminals have banking and visa facilities, but queues can be long at peak times.

Most European and American nationals can get a visa upon arrival by going to the bank before passport control and paying for the stamps needed for their visa, then proceeding to passport control where the visa is then issued. It's a good idea to get some change for the taxi driver's or porter's tip at the same time. There are taxis, buses and 'Misr Travel' coaches from the airport, though the easiest option is to take a fixed-rate limousine or taxi, booked and prepaid at the airport.

If your plane departs between 8am and 10pm, allow at least 1½ hours to get from central Cairo to the airport.

Alexandria, Aswan, Hurghada, Luxor and Sharm al-Shaykh also have airports. These handle domestic flights from Cairo as well as many international charter flights from Western Europe.

B

BICYCLE HIRE

You can hire a bicycle at Luxor and Aswan, on either bank of the Nile. Cycling is a relaxing way to visit the various tombs and ruins, or to appreciate the landscape of the Nile Valley.

Bicycles can be rented for about 20–30LE a day. Before you set off, check your bike carefully and test ride it to make sure it works properly. No crash helmets or other safety equipment are available.

BUDGETING FOR YOUR TRIP

Air fare: London–Cairo from £300, New York–Cairo from $1,000
Charter: London–Luxor/Sharm al-Shaykh £149–225 (return)
Air fare: Cairo–Luxor $100–120
Air fare: Aswan–Abu Simbel $100–120 (includes tour and transfers)
Room per night in moderate hotel: $60–100
Dinner per person in moderate restaurant: 120–180LE
Entrance fee to Giza Pyramids: 60LE
Sound-and-light show: 100LE
Entrance fee to Egyptian Museum: 60LE
Camel ride at the pyramids: official price 25LE/hour
Taxi fare, Cairo–airport: 100LE (double at night and rush hours)
Daily taxi rental: from 750LE
Windsurf rental: 200LE per day/80LE per hour
Horseback-riding: 80LE per hour

C

CAMPING

There are camping facilities along the Nile Valley, at the oases, along the Mediterranean and Red Sea coasts and at Sinai's coastal resorts, but they are barely cheaper than an inexpensive hotel. Contact the Egyptian Tourist Authority (see TOURIST INFORMATION) for a list.

CAR HIRE

Car hire in Egypt is expensive, and driving once there can be diffi-cult (see DRIVING). Cairo's road system and the habits of the dri-vers make it difficult to navigate, and taxis, which are plentiful and cheap, are a much better bet. Following the terrorist attacks in the late 1990s, foreigners are not permitted to travel independently be-tween towns and cities along the Nile Valley and across to the Red Sea. A system of convoys has been devised to give military protec-tion to foreign travellers, whether on guided tours or going it alone. Tourists travelling by car must work within the convoy timetable and should report to the local police station to liaise with them.

Sinai is one area that can still be seen by rental car or by taxi. Roads are generally quiet and in good condition, but driving after dark is not recommended.

You can hire a car from Cairo Airport or from major hotels in the capital. In the Red Sea and Sinai resorts car-hire companies have offices along the main streets. Be aware that vehicles may not be new and may have had previous damage, so check them thorough-ly before driving away. Most short-term rental contracts will be 'lim-ited kilometres' only, so try to estimate how many kilometres you will drive in order to arrive at an overall price.

Always check the small print on contracts and find out who is responsible for damage should an accident occur. Many companies have high damage excesses. The international companies work under franchise in Egypt; for your peace of mind you may prefer to book through them before you travel so that you can discuss and agree on the clauses of the rental's small print.

Drivers must be aged at least 21 and must be in possession of a full national driving licence or international licence. It is general-ly better to pay for car hire with a credit card, otherwise you will have to put down a very large cash deposit.

Avis: Cairo International Airport, tel: 02-2654249; Hurghada, tel: 065-3447400; <www.avisegypt.com>

CLIMATE

October, November, April and May are the best months to visit Egypt. Summers can be stifling, especially in Upper Egypt, with temperatures well over 37°C (100°F). It is also hot in the Sinai and along the Red Sea coast. Most hotels, tour buses and Nile cruise ships have air-conditioning, but you should do your sightseeing in the morning or the evening to avoid the worst of the sun.

Winter is mostly warm in Upper Egypt, with daytime temperatures still rising to the mid-20s °C (upper 70s °F). Evenings can be chilly, especially in the Sinai where night frost is not unknown. Cairo and the north have temperatures in the low-20s °C (upper 60s °C) in winter. Again evenings can feel chilly. Rain is rare in Egypt – only Alexandria and the Mediterranean coast see a measurable amount, and occasionally also Cairo. The Red Sea and Sinai coastlines benefit from sea breezes in summer, which can develop into quite strong winds in winter. The chart below shows average monthly temperatures, in centigrade, for both Cairo and Alexandria.

	J	F	M	A	M	J	J	A	S	O	N	D
Cairo	14	15	18	21	23	27	29	28	26	24	20	15
Alexandria	14	15	16	19	22	24	26	27	25	23	20	16

CLOTHING

If you are visiting Egypt between May and September, take light, loose-fitting cotton clothing. Always carry sunglasses (the sandstone monuments along the Nile can be surprisingly bright in the sunshine) and take a hat to protect against sun stroke. In winter, take extra layers for the evenings. You will also need warm clothes if you are climbing Mount Sinai and for nights in the desert, whatever the season.

Shoes for sightseeing should be flat, comfortable and sturdy enough to take all the uneven surfaces. Heels should be reserved for dinner only. In large 5-star hotels and on certain Nile cruise vessels you may be asked to dress smart-casual (ie jacket and tie for men) in the evenings.

When visiting mosques, men should wear trousers and a shirt; women should also cover their arms and legs, and preferably have a headscarf to hand. Everyone must remove their shoes.

COMPLAINTS

In the first instance you should take up your grievance with the management of the organisation concerned. If you are still not satisfied, contact the Tourist Police or the local police at your location (see POLICE). They are usually co-operative.

Many tourist complaints stem from overcharging in taxis, cafés and bars. In a country where there are few set prices, it is therefore always advisable to check the price before you order.

CRIME AND SAFETY

Egypt is, by and large, a law-abiding country with very few serious crimes committed against visitors. Recent terrorist attacks against tourists were carried out by religious extremists and do not indicate a general dislike of visitors amongst the general population. The Egyptian government now controls tourist travel along the Nile Valley in Upper Egypt and from the Nile Valley to the Red Sea. However, petty crime is rising, especially in the more popular tourist areas and crowded places such as the markets. To avoid becoming a victim of crime, take the following precautions:
• Never carry large amounts of cash.
• Leave all valuables in the hotel safe.
• Guard bags and pockets, especially in crowded areas.
• Always walk in well-lit streets at night.
• Do not leave valuables on the beach when you swim.
• Keep photocopies of important paperwork, such as airline tickets, and passport and traveller's cheque numbers.

CUSTOMS AND ENTRY REQUIREMENTS

Visas. All visitors to Egypt need a transit visa for stays of up to seven days or a tourist visa for stays not exceeding one month (but extendable for up to six months). These are supplied by the Egyptian embassy in your home country or at the airport upon arrival. The cost of a visa is US $20 (foreign currency only). It will allow you to travel in all areas of Egypt.

If you are travelling overland from Israel, you cannot get a visa on the Israel-Egypt border. You should instead obtain a visa beforehand from Tel Aviv or from the consulate in Eilat. A 'Sinai only' visa allows you to travel freely around the peninsula, but not into mainland Egypt. Because of ongoing problems within Israel, do check the travel situation between the two countries before you depart.

Customs. If you are travelling with expensive cameras, video or computer equipment, it is advisable to declare them upon entry into the country. Details will be noted; you will then be asked to produce the equipment on your departure, to prove you have not sold anything during your stay. Prohibited items are drugs, firearms and cotton.

All visitors may bring the following items into Egypt duty-free:
- 200 cigarettes or 25 cigars or 200g of tobacco.
- 1 litre of alcohol but you can buy another 3 litres of alcohol within 24 hours of arrival in one of the Egypt Free shops.
- 1 litre of perfume.
- Gifts to the value of 500LE.

Currency restrictions. No more than 1,000LE may be exported but the import of local currency is unlimited. Any amount of foreign currency may be imported or exported but it must be declared on entry. Customs will stamp the currency declaration form on entry. Keep it, along with all currency exchange receipts: you may have to show them on your departure.

D

DRIVING

As a result of the terrorist attacks around Luxor in Upper Egypt in the late 1990s, security systems have been put in place to minimise the risk to tourists. All tourist travel is controlled and a system of convoys with military guards operates in Upper Egypt. If you book a tour with a company then all arrangements will all be taken care of. However, if you wish to travel independently (by hire car or taxi) you must report to the police who will tell you the time of the convoys. Travelling by convoy means you cannot stop along the convoy route or make any interesting detours.

The convoy system covers the following routes along the Nile Valley in Upper Egypt: from Luxor north (including Denderah and Abydos temples); from Aswan to Luxor and vice versa; Luxor to Hurghada and vice versa; and west of Luxor into the desert.

Road conditions. Road conditions are improving, with good routes north from Cairo to Alexandria, and throughout Sinai. The main Nile Valley route on the east bank is undergoing improvement; its condition varies enormously from one stretch to the next, and care should be taken at all times.

Most drivers don't seem to obey any rules, so be alert at all times. Overtaking is done in the face of oncoming traffic, and cars pull on and off the highway without indicating. Small buses weave in and out of traffic lanes, often stopping to pick up passengers. Vehicles that in many countries would be deemed unfit for the road circulate freely in Egypt.

Rules of the road. In theory Egyptians drive on the right and pass on the left, though in practice anything goes. Speed limits are 100km/hr (62mph) on dual highways and 90km/hr (56mph) on other roads, unless otherwise indicated.

Road signs. Road signs are rare, and distance signs are not always completely accurate.

Fuel. Fuel is inexpensive and sold by the litre. Most modern gas pumps give price and quantity in Roman rather than Arabic numerals so you can see how much you are buying and at what price.

Parking. Finding a place to park in Cairo is a challenge. Most large hotels have a garage, but clients may be charged for its use.

Breakdown and assistance. There are no breakdown services in Egypt, but in case of breakdown or accident you can call the Red Crescent, which operates a network of garages across the country. Ask for their telephone number when you rent the vehicle. For more information on assistance, contact the Automobile Club of Egypt, 10 Sharia Qasr an-Nil, Cairo, tel: 02-574 3355.

E

ELECTRICITY

Egypt operates on 220 volts and 50 hertz with the exception of Alexandria, Heliopolis and Maadi, which use 110 volts and 50 hertz. Plugs are the two-pin round variety, as in Europe. Note that the electricity supply in Egypt is prone to interruptions and variations in current, so there are occasional blackouts. You will usually find a candle and matches in hotel rooms for such eventualities.

EMBASSIES AND CONSULATES

Australia: World Trade Centre, 11th floor, 1191 Corniche an-Nil, Bulaq, Cairo; tel: 02-5750444; <www.dfat.gov.au/missions>

Canada: 26 Kamel al-Shenawy, Garden City, Cairo; PO Box 1667; tel: 02-7943110; email: <cairo@dfait-maeci.gc.ca>

Republic of Ireland: 3 Abu al-Feda Street, 7th floor, Zamalek, Cairo; PO Box 2681; tel: 02-7358547; email: <irishemb@rite.com>

South Africa: 55 Road 18, Maadi, Cairo; tel: 02-3594952/75; <www.dfa.gov.za>

UK (and New Zealand): 7 Ahmed Ragheb Street, Garden City, Cairo, Tel: 02-7940850–8; <www.britishembassy.org.eg>

US: 8 Kamal el Din Salah Street, Garden City, Cairo; tel: 02-7973300/01; <www.usembassy.egnet.net>

EMERGENCIES (See also CRIME AND SAFETY)

In case of an emergency, telephone:
Ambulance **123**
Cairo Tourist Police **126**
Fire **180**
Police **122**

G

GAY AND LESBIAN TRAVELLERS

Egypt is an Islamic country with conservative values. There is no openly gay scene, and close physical contact in public, whether between heterosexual or same-sex couples, is frowned upon. In recent years there have been incidents of gay men being arrested in Cairo and later imprisoned.

GETTING THERE

Egypt Air (<www.egyptair.com.eg>) is the national carrier for Egypt and it operates a network of international services to London, Manchester, New York, Los Angeles, Cape Town, Johannesburg and Sydney. They also operate services to and from

Amsterdam, Frankfurt, Milan, Geneva, Paris and Rome. For connection to Australia and New Zealand, Egypt Air operates a service to Singapore.

The following European airlines also fly to Cairo: British Airways (<www.britishairways.com>), KLM (<www.klm.com>), Lufthansa (<www.lufthansa.com>), Air France (<www.airfrance. com>) and Iberia (<www.iberia.com>).

Connections to Europe from North America for onward travel to Cairo can be made with Northwest Airlines (<www.nwa.com>), Air Canada (<www.aircanada.ca>), Continental Airlines (<www.continental.com>), Delta Airlines (<www.delta.com>), American Airlines (<www.aa.com>) and Virgin Atlantic (<www.virgin-atlantic.com>).

From Australia and New Zealand you can reach Europe for onward flights to Cairo with Singapore Airlines (<www.singaporeair.com>), Thai Airways (<www.thaiair.com>), Qantas (<www. qantas.com>) and Air New Zealand (<www.airnewzealand.co.nz>).

If you want a pre-booked itinerary for your trip, visit an experienced travel agent in North America who can advise on the myriad inclusive tours or customised options available.

Several firms offer package holidays to Cairo, the Nile Valley, Sinai and the Red Sea, notably Kuoni (<www.kuoni.co.uk>), Thomas Cook (<www.thomascook.com>) and Soliman Travel (<www.solimantravel.co.uk>).

GUIDES AND TOURS

The resorts and towns have a wealth of travel agencies who can organise tours of the nearby sites. Check prices and what is included before booking. Only officially approved guides are allowed to accompany tourists to archaeological sites. To find one, ask at your hotel, a travel agent or the Egyptian Tourist Authority (see page 125). A guide can be very useful when visiting the Valley of the Kings or Cairo's mosques.

There is a good network of tourist excursions from every town and if you have not already pre-booked you will be able to arrange these on arrival. Prices will be in US dollars, but note that not all travel agents accept credit cards, so you may need to pay in cash.

H

HEALTH AND MEDICAL CARE

No inoculations are needed at present, but it's best to check with your doctor before travelling. Malaria exists in the Al-Fayyoum and Delta regions. Rabies is present in Egypt, so be wary of animals. The most common ailments for tourists are dehydration and upset stomachs. Take the following precautions to minimise the risks:

• Drink plenty of bottled water and always carry a supply with you. Do not drink tap water and avoid ice in drinks.

• Do not drink the Nile water, swim in it, or walk barefoot along its banks: the water contains bilharzia, a parasitic flatworm.

• Go easy on alcohol, as this will increase the effects of dehydration.

• Wash your hands before eating.

• Eat well-cooked meat and peel fruit before eating it.

• If you eat at buffets, ensure that cold dishes have been well-chilled and hot dishes have been freshly cooked.

• Be aware that milk and dairy products may be unpasteurised in non-tourist establishments.

Pharmacies (agzakhána or saydaliya) have a green crescent sign decorated with a red cross or serpent. Local medicines may not have the same names as at home. Check with the hotel doctor before buying anything you are not sure about.

Doctors and hospitals. Large hotels have English-speaking doctors on call. The Anglo-American Hospital in Cairo is west of the Cairo Tower on Gazirah Island (tel: 02-7356162); the As-Salam International Hospital is on Corniche an-Nil in Maadi (tel: 02 524 0077).

HITCHHIKING

Hitchhiking is not recommended. Moreover, with the new security measures for foreign travellers following the terrorist attacks in the 1990s, it would be difficult to hitch, as all travel involving tourists is controlled in central Egypt. Bus fares north of Cairo (towards Alexandria) are very reasonable. Travel from Luxor to Aswan, and from Luxor across to the Red Sea is controlled by the Egyptian military.

HOLIDAYS

There are six secular holidays in Egypt, when banks, government offices, many businesses and schools are closed:

1 January	New Year (banks only)
First Monday after Coptic Easter	Sham an-Nasim (Spring Festival)
25 April	Sinai Liberation Day
1 May	Labour Day
23 July	Revolution Day
6 October	Armed Forces Day

All Muslim holidays are celebrated in Egypt but shops are not necessarily closed. At **Ramadan** (dates change each year; *see page* 97), when the Muslim population fasts during daylight hours, offices are open fewer hours, and shops close in the afternoon but remain open well into the night. Most restaurants stop selling alcohol, though not major hotels. Note that as the Islamic day starts at sunset most celebrations begin the night before the actual date.

L

LANGUAGE

Arabic is the official language of Egypt, and Egyptian Arabic is widely understood around the Arabic-speaking world, where there are many regional 'dialects'. Most people working in the tourist industry speak some English, though less so away from the main towns. You will often find local people, particularly children, practising a handful of English phrases on you.

hello, welcome	ahlan wa sahlan
good morning	sabáh-il-kheyr
good evening	masáal-kheyr
goodbye	ma'a-saláama
yes/no	aywa/laa'a
please/thank you	minfadlak/shukran
What is your name? (to a male)	íssmak eh?
What is your name? (to a female)	íssmik eh?
How are you? (to a male)	izzáyak
How are you? (to a female)	izzáyik
I am fine.	kwayiss (M), kwayíssa (F)
thank God	il-hamdu li-lah

M

MAPS

The Egyptian Tourist Authority (see page 125) issues basic maps for all the towns, and some hotels distribute maps free of charge. Most towns are easy to explore but Cairo can be relatively difficult. Hiring a guide is a good option: they can take you to all the major attractions and introduce you to some less known districts of the capital.

MEDIA

Newspapers. *The Egyptian Gazette* and the *Daily Star* are published daily in English giving up-to-date news from around world, concentrating on Egypt and the Middle East. *Al-Ahram Weekly* is an excellent English-language newspaper focused on Egypt and the Middle East. International newspapers are available at newsstands in major hotels, though some may be a day old.

TV and radio. Egypt has three television channels. Channel II has daily news bulletins in English. Major hotels have satellite TV with CNN, BBC News 24 and English-language entertainment channels.

There are two national radio stations; FM95 transmits news in English at 2.30pm and 8pm.

MONEY

Currency. Egypt's monetary unit is the Egyptian pound (*guineh* in Arabic), abbreviated to LE. This is divided into 100 piastres (pt). Bank notes are issued in denominations of 50pt, 1LE, 5LE, 10LE, 20LE, 50LE, 100LE and 200LE, while coins are available in units of 10pt, 20pt and 25pt.

Currency exchange. Foreign currency must be exchanged with an official organisation; this may be a bank or official exchange office. Most large hotels have a small bank on the premises, open in the mornings and evenings. The exchange rate is more favourable within Egypt so take minimal amounts with you into the country. Always obtain receipts for your transactions, as they may be checked on your exit from Egypt. Street banks are open from 8am–1pm Mon–Thurs. Exchange booths work longer hours and give a slightly better rate.

Credit cards. These are becoming more widely accepted in restaurants and shops. All major hotels will accept them in payment for rooms and services. You can use your credit card to obtain cash at banks with a small additional service charge. Take your passport and expect to wait for some time as security checks are made.

ATMs. Cash dispensers are increasingly commonplace. The major towns have numerous ATMs, and most big hotels in Cairo have one in the lobby, but there are very few in the countryside or the oases.

Traveller's cheques. Banks and hotels will accept these, but you cannot use them to buy goods in shops, even in the big towns.

OPENING HOURS

Banks are open Monday to Thursday from 8am–1pm, though the smaller official bank offices in large hotels are usually also open in the evenings to facilitate money-changing.

Post offices. Cairo's main post office is at Ataba Square. It is open 24 hours a day except on Fridays when it is open 7am–noon. Other post offices open from 8.30am–3pm Saturday to Thursday, and from 8.30am–11.30am on Fridays.

Administration. Government offices generally open Mon–Fri 9am–5pm, with a break from 11.30am–1.30pm on Friday. Airline offices remain open until 8pm.

Shops. In Cairo, shops are open 9am–7pm in winter and 9am–8pm in summer, some closing one hour later on Mondays and Thursdays all year round. Government shops are closed 2–5pm for the siesta, and private shops may also close at hours to suit their owners. The big bazaar, Khan al-Khalili, is open until 8pm every day except

Sunday. In other tourist towns private shops open daily and stay open until late – often around 10pm. During Ramadan, shops are often open later – some until after midnight, but they always close for 30 minutes at sunset to take the fast-breaking *iftar* meal.

Museums and archaeological sites. Major museums and sites are open daily from 8am until 5pm. Smaller museums may be open in the mornings only. Some sites, such as Luxor, stay open until 10pm. Those with sound-and-light shows will restrict admittance in the evenings to a small number of ticket holders. Most sites curtail opening hours during Ramadan.

P

POLICE

The main police station in Cairo is at 5 Adly Street, downtown Cairo.

In case of problems, telephone:
Police *(bolís)* **122**
Cairo Tourist Police **126**

POST OFFICES

The postal service in Egypt is slow and unpredictable. If you want to send a package or something important or urgent it is better to send it by courier; several of the major international companies have offices in the country.

Postboxes have no set colour, so you are better off using the facilities at your hotel – or any major hotel – to send your postcards. These take at least 14 days to reach Europe, and 18 days further afield.

Cairo's main post office is at Ataba Square. It is open 24 hours a day except on Fridays, when it is open 7am–noon. Opening times for other post offices are from 8.30am–3pm Saturday to Thursday, and from 8.30am–11.30am on Fridays.

R

RELIGION

Egypt is a predominantly Muslim country, with a Coptic Christian minority of nearly 10 percent and a tiny Jewish population.

Courtesy requires that visitors should dress modestly, and greet, shake hands and eat with the right hand. You should refrain from showing the sole of your feet or shoes when sitting on the ground. Always remove your shoes when visiting a mosque.

Muslims fast during the month of Ramadan, refraining from eating during daylight hours. Many restaurants stay closed during the day or may serve special dishes rather than a full menu. Only tourist hotels and a few restaurants will serve alcohol during this period. At all times of the year, respect Islamic tradition by not drinking alcohol in public, except in tourist-orientated bars and restaurants.

T

TELEPHONES

The majority of public telephones in Aswan, Hurghada, Luxor and Sharm al-Shaykh accept phone cards rather than coins. Phone cards are issued in units of 5, 10, 20 and 40. For international calls you will need one with 20 or 40 units. Post offices also have phone booths where you can make international calls and pay at the end (there's a 3-minute minimum charge). Most large hotels have direct-dial international lines. They add huge surcharges to the cost of the call, but connections are often more reliable. It is more economical to use your credit card or a pre-pay international card with an international access number.

Egypt's telephone system is in the process of being upgraded, and codes and numbers are therefore subject to change. To check a number dial 140; most operators speak some English. The international code for Egypt is 20. Each town has an area code prefix, which you omit if you are calling within the same town or area. Examples are: 03 for Alexandria, 097 for Aswan, 02 for Cairo, 065 for Hurghada and the Red Sea coast, 095 for Luxor, 062 for Sinai. The codes 010 and 012 denote mobile (cell) phones.

International country codes are as follows, all prefixed by 00 when you make a call: Australia 61, South Africa 27, Canada 1, United Kingdom 44, Ireland 353, United States 1 and New Zealand 64.

TIME ZONES

Egypt operates on GMT +2 hours. Clocks go forward one hour during the summer.

TIPPING

In Egypt, the practice of tipping, or *baksheesh*, is widespread. Children and beggars may approach you in the street asking for *baksheesh*. Although you don't need to give them money, it is a good idea to carry plenty of small banknotes to give to those who provide a service. The following people will expect tips:

Porter	4–8LE per bag
Waiter	10 percent if service not incl.
Toilet attendant	5LE
Maid	60–100LE per week
Taxi driver	1–5LE
Tour guide	10 percent
Cruise guide	50–100LE per client
Felucca boatman	10–20LE per passenger

TOILETS

Good toilet facilities *(toualét)* are generally found in all the large hotels and museums. Restaurants have toilets, though hygiene standards vary and you should buy a drink if you want to use their facilities.

TOURIST INFORMATION

The **Egyptian Tourist Authority** (ETA) is an excellent resource. For information before you travel, you can visit their official website at <www.touregypt.net>; <www.egypttourism.org> is a further official site for visitors from America.

You can also visit their offices at the following addresses:

UK
3rd Floor, Egyptian House
170 Piccadilly
London W1V 9DD
Tel: 020 7493 5282

US
630 Fifth Avenue, Suite 1706
New York, NY 10111
Tel: 212-3322570

Canada
1253 McGill College Avenue #250
Montreal
Québec H3B 2Y5
Tel: 514-8614420

For tourist information offices within Egypt, the Egyptian Tourist Authority is based at the following:
Cairo: 5 Adly Street, tel: 02-3913454. You will also find smaller offices at the pyramids and at Cairo International Airport.
Alexandria: Saad Zaghoul Square, tel: 03-4851556.
Luxor: Tourist Bazaar, Corniche an-Nil, tel: 095-2372215.
Aswan: Midan al-Mahatta, tel: 097-2312811.
Hurghada: Bank Misr Street, tel: 065-3444420.

TRANSPORT

Boats. To get across the Nile at Luxor and Aswan use *felluca* sail-boats, or the faster and cheaper diesel-engined ferries that work to a regular timetable. Four days a week there is also a high-speed ferry which takes 90 minutes to do the crossing from Hurghada to Sharm al-Shaykh (vehicles accepted).

Buses. Buses are over-crowded in Cairo and often driven at speed along complicated routes. Several good air-conditioned services a day link Cairo with Alexandria and other towns in Egypt.

Horse-drawn carriages. You can hire these (also called *calèches*) in Luxor, Aswan and elsewhere in the Nile Valley – there are even some in Cairo for those daring enough to brave the roads in one.

Metro. The excellent Cairo metro links several parts of the city through Tahrir Square. Most useful for the visitor is the route to the Coptic museum and Old Cairo. For this you should get off at Mari Girgis Station.

Minibuses. The air-conditioned minibuses with limited seats are an easier way to get around Cairo.

Planes. Egypt Air (tel: 02-5750600, <www.egyptair.com.eg>) operates domestic flights from Cairo to Abu Simbel, Alexandria, Aswan, Hurghada, Luxor, Marsa Matruh on the Mediterranean, New Valley (Western Desert) and Sharm al-Shaykh. You should book ahead, confirm tickets and check in at least an hour before take-off, as overbooking is frequent.

Taxis. Shared group taxis, which are plentiful across Egypt, tend to be quicker than the bus for roughly the same price. These vehicles take six or seven passengers and simply leave when they are full.

Trains. There is a frequent fast service between Cairo and Alexandria. Services down the Nile are reliable, but enquire whether foreign travellers may use them, as they are not always guarded. An overnight luxury train operates to and from Luxor/Aswan; cabins must be pre-booked, and prices are expensive; contact Wagons-lit (tel: 02-5749274, <www.sleepingtrains.com>) in front of Ramesses Station, Cairo.

WEBSITES

The following sites will give you general information about Egypt:
• <www.touregypt.net> Official site of Egyptian Tourist Authority.
• <www.egypttourism.org> Egyptian Tourist Authority in America.
• <www.discoveregypt.co.uk> UK-based commercial website.
• <www.red-sea.com> Information on diving and other watersports.
• <www.cairocafe.com> Listings of what's on in Cairo.
• <www.cairotourist.com> Virtual travel guide.
• <www.luxorguide.com> For information on Luxor.
• <http://weekly.ahram.org.eg> Website of the excellent English-language weekly paper.

WEIGHTS AND MEASURES

Egypt uses the metric system for weights and measures.

YOUTH HOSTELS *(beit shabáb)*

There are youth hostels in Cairo and Alexandria, but the quality varies, and the best are fully booked well in advance. You should always pre-book. Contact the International Youth Hotel Association in your own country or see <www.yha.org> for further information and advice.

Recommended Hotels

Egypt has numerous hotels, but good establishments in the lower price brackets are still fairly rare. Tariffs are lower for Egyptians than for foreign visitors, who are usually asked to pay in US dollars, particularly in the better hotels, although some do accept Egyptian pounds (LE). To take advantage of lower prices and promotions, it is best to pre-book, especially in the better-class hotels. Luxury hotels add a 12 percent service charge to bills. A municipal tax of 2 percent and a sales tax of 5 percent are added to all hotel bills. Major credit cards are widely accepted.

The list below includes hotels in a range of categories in all the major tourist towns, plus a recommendation for a Nile cruise. The symbols ($) indicate the approximate cost of a double room for one night.

$$$$$	above $160
$$$$	$120–160
$$$	$80–120
$$	$40–80
$	below $40

It is generally best to confirm a reservation by fax or email. To contact hotels from outside Egypt dial 20 and the regional code.

ALEXANDRIA AND THE MEDITERRANEAN

Four Seasons Alexandria $$$$$ *399 Tariq El Geish, San Stefano, tel: 03-4690141, <www.fourseasons.com/alexandria>*. The new five-star hotel in town, and by far the most luxurious hotel in Alexandria, the Four Seasons overlooks the Mediterranean and San Stefano Beach. The rooms and suites are spacious and elegant, and each has a private balcony with sea views. The hotel also boasts a European-style spa, excellent restaurants and an upmarket shopping mall.

Paradise Inn-Metropole $$$ *52 Saad Zaghoul Street, Alexandria, tel: 03-4861467, <www.paradiseinegypt.com>*. A beautiful early

20th-century hotel decorated throughout in Louis XIV style – the huge heavy doors, wallpapered ceilings and heavy drapes of the ornate communal areas could almost have come from a French château. Situated on the main square in the city, it is ideally located for touring. Rooms of differing sizes are all well-furnished; those at the rear have sea views. Rooms have air-conditioning, TV and phone. Facilities include a good Egyptian restaurant. 30 rooms. Major credit cards.

Sofitel Cecil $$$$ *Saad Zaghloul Square, Alexandria, tel: 03-4877173, fax: 03-4855655, <www.sofitel.com>.* This central, old-style hotel, featured in Durrell's *Alexandria Quartet*, commands sweeping views over the Eastern Harbour. Notable guests have included Agatha Christie, Josephine Baker, Omar Sharif and Field Marshall Montgomery. Rooms are updated but unatmospheric, and have air-conditioning, satellite TV, mini-bar, hairdryer and private balconies. Non-smoking rooms are available. Facilities include a fitness room with sauna and massage, a bookshop, bank, hairdresser, car-hire service, business centre, 5 restaurants, Monty's bar, a nightclub, disco and casino. 86 rooms. Major credit cards.

Union $ *164 Shari' 26 July Street, 5th Floor, Alexandria, tel: 03-4807312, fax: 03-4807350.* The Union offers sweeping views over the sea and the bay of Alexandria, and its sea-facing lounge is a wonderful place for an afternoon drink. Comfortable and clean rooms.

ASWAN

Basma $$–$$$ *Abtal at-Tahrir Street, Aswan, tel: 097-2310901, <www.basmahotel.com>.* A modern and clean resort hotel built at the top of the hill, on the Nile, near the Nubian Museum. Great views from the Nile-side rooms and garden terraces. All rooms are equipped with air-conditioning, satellite TV, mini-bar and balconies. Other guest services include 24-hour room service, shopping arcade, clinic, 3 restaurants and several bars, and a large swimming pool. Friendly staff. 189 rooms.

Sofitel Old Cataract $$$$ *Abtal at-Tahrir Street, Aswan, tel: 097-2316000, <www.sofitel.com>*. Harking back to the days of elegant Edwardian Grand Tours, the Old Cataract Hotel has become a landmark in Aswan and has seen such illustrious guests as Winston Churchill and Agatha Christie, who wrote *Death on the Nile* while staying here. The Nile looks wonderful from the hotel's elegant terrace and gardens. Ask for a room with a river view. Rooms have air-conditioning, satellite TV, phone and tea and coffee. Facilities include an excellent restaurant, pool, bar and parking. Buffet breakfast is compulsory and charged to your bill. 131 rooms. Major credit cards.

CAIRO

Cosmopolitan $$ *1 Ibn Taalab Street, Cairo, tel: 02-3923663/7522, fax: 02-3933531*. This Art Deco hotel is situated downtown in the recently rejuvenated area of the old Bourse (Stock Exchange). The hotel has been renovated without losing any of its belle époque character. All the architectural details remain, and the simple rooms are furnished in period style. An interesting option for budget travellers, as it has more charm than many others at a comparable price. Rooms have TV and phone. Facilities include restaurant, café, bar and business centre. 84 rooms. Major credit cards.

Four Seasons at Nile Plaza $$$$$ *1089 Corniche al-Nil, Garden City, tel: 02-7917000, <www.fourseasons.com>*. One of the most luxurious and sumptuous hotels in Cairo, part of the exclusive Nile Plaza, the most expensive real estate in town. The vast rooms have air-conditioning, satellite TV, mini-bar, hairdryer and magnificent views over the Nile. Non-smoking rooms are available. Facilities include 24-hour room service, gym, spa, pool and several excellent restaurants. 365 rooms. Major credit cards.

Garden City House $ *23, Shari'Kamal ad-Din Salah, Garden City, Cairo, tel: 02-5420600, <www.gardencityhouse.com>*. This pleasant, if slightly dusty, pension, is popular with scholars and archaeologists. It has good-sized, clean rooms, some of which overlook the Nile. Very good value for money.

Hotel Luna $ *5th floor, 27 Sharia Talaat Harb, tel: 02-3961020,* *<www.hotellunacairo.com>.* Very popular, clean and pleasant hotel in the heart of Cairo. The hotel has a breakfast room, a Beduin-style café with *sheeshas*, internet, laundry facilities and luggage storage.

Mena House Oberoi Hotel $$$$$ *Pyramids Road, Giza, tel: 02-3833222, fax: 02-3837777, <www.oberoihotels.com>.* In this recently renovated old palace, a former royal hunting lodge, you can wake up to a magnificent close-up view of the Great Pyramids of Giza. The newer rooms, built around a beautiful, peaceful garden, have less charm, and the Pyramids are slightly further away. Rooms are equipped with all mod cons. Facilities include swimming pool, tennis, golf course, casino, nightclub and several restaurants including the Moghul Room, the best Indian restaurant in Cairo. 486 rooms. Major credit cards.

Nile Hilton $$$$ *Corniche El Nil, Cairo, tel: 02-5780444, fax: 02-5780475, <www.hilton.com>.* Perfectly located next to the Egyptian Museum and the Nile, the Nile Hilton is great if you want to explore Cairo on foot. The 430 guest rooms are spacious and comfortable, and have great views over the city or the Nile. Choose a room on a higher floor, as lower floors can be quite noisy. Five-star facilities include a large, heated swimming pool, tennis and squash courts, health club, business centre, many in-house dining options and a great shopping arcade. Breakfast extra. Major credit cards.

Semiramis Intercontinental $$$$ *Corniche El Nil, near Midan Tahrir, Cairo, tel: 02-7957171, fax 02-7963020, <www.cairo. intercontinental.com>.* On the Nile, just across busy Tahrir Square from the Egyptian Museum, this modern, 800-room five-star hotel, built in 1987, is just steps away from downtown shopping and dining. Décor is standard contemporary; with many guest rooms offering Nile views. Eleven restaurants include the outstanding Birdcage (Thai) and the Sambaya (Lebanese); there's also the best hotel dinner buffet in town. Breakfast extra. Major credit cards.

Talisman $$ *5th floor, 39 Sharia Talaat Harb, tel: 02 3939431, email: <talisman_hoteldecharme@yahoo.fr>.* A delightful small boutique hotel with individually decorated rooms in a downtown flat. All rooms have air-conditioning and private bathrooms with bathrobes. A continental breakfast is served in the Ottoman-style lobby. Major credit cards.

LUXOR

Al-Moudira $$$$$ *Daba'iyya, West Bank, Luxor, tel: 012-325 1307, <www.moudira.com>.* Upper Egypt's first boutique hotel – jewellery designer Zeina Aboukheir's Orientalist dream – is set dramatically on the edge of the desert and the lush sugarcane fields on the undeveloped west bank of the Nile, just 5km (3 miles) from the Valley of the Queens. The vast rooms are furnished with handmade Oriental furniture and treasures salvaged from old Cairo houses. You'll fnd domed ceilings, hand-painted frescoes, huge bathrooms, satellite TV, air-conditioning and phone. Facilities include a bar, a restaurant partly supplied from its own organic garden, and a beautiful swimming pool set in the garden. The perfect place to experience total relaxation. 54 rooms. Major credit cards.

Old Winter Palace $$$$ *Khalid Ibn al-Waleed Street, Luxor, tel: 095-2380422, email: <h1661@accor-hotels.com>.* The grande dame of Luxor hotels, built on the banks of the Nile in 1886, the Winter Palace still makes a statement with its facade of rosy-coloured stucco work. The interior is expansive and rooms have lofty ceilings and French-style windows. Updated and modernised in 1994, it is still best enjoyed for its period charm. Ask for a room with a river view. Rooms have air-conditioning, satellite TV, phone and minibar. Facilities include a large heated pool, tennis and squash courts, gardens, two restaurants, coffee shop, shops and entertainment. Free airport transfer. 136 rooms. Major credit cards.

Nour al-Balad $$ *Ezbet Bisilly, left at the turning for the Valley of the Queens, tel: 02-2426111.* Wonderful mud-brick hotel on the edge of the fertile land and the desert, overlooking the Thebes mountains. The rooms are spacious and stylishly decorated with local furniture, including beds made out of palm wood. A great breakfast is served in the garden, and if you wake up early you can see hot air balloons land nearby. A very peaceful hotel, perfect to stay a little while longer and sightsee on the west bank at a more leisurely pace.

St Joseph $ *Khaled Ibn al-Walid Street, Luxor, tel: 095-2381707, fax: 095-381727, email: <sjhiey2002@hotmail.com>.* A good budget option, the St Joseph is clean and nicely furnished. Situated a five-minute walk south of the Corniche on the main street, it is surrounded by several larger, more expensive hotels and a range of Egyptian eateries. Rooms have air-conditioning, phone, TV and balcony, and many have Nile views. Facilities include restaurant, bar, rooftop pool and shop. 75 rooms. Major credit cards.

RED SEA AND SINAI

Al-Khan $$$ *In the al-Gouna resort, 20km (12 miles) north of Hurghada, tel: 065-3580052/3, fax: 065-3549712, <www.elgouna.com>.* A lovely hotel with domed rooms and arches, in a style influenced by the Egyptian architect Hassan Fathy and set around Arab-style courtyards. The rooms have air-conditioning, mini-bar, satellite TV and direct phone lines. There is a restaurant, and guests have access to the private beach and pool. 25 rooms. Major credit cards.

Four Seasons $$$$$ *15km (9 miles) north of Na'ama Bay, Sharm al-Shaykh, Sinai, tel: 069-3603555, fax: 069-3603550, <www.fourseasons.com>.* One of the newest and most luxurious resorts in a quiet bay near the resort strip of Na'ama. The hotel is built in an Oriental style with a relatively small number of rooms. All rooms have balconies, and most have sea views, CD player, hairdryer, safe, mini-bar, satellite TV, air-conditioning and DVD player. Facilities include 3 pools plus small pools that come with the suites, whirlpools, five excellent restaurants, spa, tennis courts, shopping centre, children's club, diving and other watersports facilities. 136 rooms. Major credit cards.

Nesima Resort $$$ *Mashraba, Dahab, tel: 069-3640320, <www. nesima-resort.com>.* One of Sinai's funkiest hotels, built in traditional style and offering very good value for money. The domed rooms have bathroom, air-conditioning and mini-bar. The rooms are constructed in small clusters around the landscaped gardens and pool area, which is in the shape of a rounded hourglass. The hotel has an excellent dive centre, a good beach restaurant plus a rooftop restaurant, the latter turning into a lively dance floor at night. Major credit cards.

Oberoi Sahl Hasheesh $$$$$ *P.O. Box 117, Hurghada, Red Sea, tel: 065-3440777, <www.oberoihotels.com>.* This suites-only resort hotel is one of the newest, and without a doubt the smartest, on the Red Sea coast. The elegant décor has rich elements of traditional Islamic design, and the rooms are beautifully appointed. Each suite has its own private courtyard, some including private swimming pool. Expansive gardens and attentive service make the Sahl Hasheesh the ideal place to recharge your spiritual and physical batteries. Suites have living rooms, air-conditioning, satellite TV, phones, computer-points, safes, mini-bars and tea- and coffee-making facilities. Amenities include private beach, pool, gourmet restaurant, bar, library, massage rooms and sauna. 104 suites. Major credit cards.

Sanafir $$$ *Na'ama Bay, Sharm al-Shaykh, tel: 069-3600197, <www.sanafirhotel.com>.* The Sanafir is the heart and soul of Na'ama Bay, one of its oldest hotels but also the most buzzing night place. The characterful rooms have air-conditioning, private bathroom/shower, mini-bar, safe-box, satellite TV and 24-hour room service. The hotel's large open-air courtyard has a Beduin tent, a rock swimming pool with waterfall, a diving centre, House Nation parties, 5 restaurants and four bar-discos. Major credit cards.

Sheraton Miramar $$$$ *Al-Gouna, 20km (12 miles) north of Hurghada, tel: 065-3545606, fax: 065-3545608, <www.star woodhotels.com>.* This luxurious fairytale hotel, designed by the celebrated architect Michael Graves, blends Nubian and Oriental styles with the beautiful surroundings of the Red Sea and the neighbouring lagoons. The brightly decorated rooms all feature terraces, air-conditioning, mini-bar and satellite TV. Facilities here include a handful of pools, a diving centre, a water-ski school, 8 restaurants and a shopping arcade. 327 rooms. Major credit cards.

SIWA OASIS

Adrére Amellal $$$$$ *Sidi Jaafar, Siwa, tel: 02-7367879, email: <info@eqi.com.eg>*. This eco-lodge is a desert retreat set in its own oasis, without electricity or phone. Built in simple mud brick mixed with salt crystals, the traditional building material, the architecture is dramatic and intricate at the same time, and the landscape stunning. At night the hotel is lit with lanterns and candles. The gourmet food from the organic garden is served on the family china, and the swimming pool is a delightful Roman well. Rates, which include all meals, drinks and desert excursions, must be paid in Cairo – no money changes hands on site. Strongly recommended. 32 very unique rooms.

NILE CRUISES

Oberoi Nile Cruises $$$$$ *Regional sales office, Mena House Oberoi, Pyramids Road, Giza, Cairo, tel: 02-3833222, fax: 02-3833444, <www.oberoihotels.com>*. The Oberoi group operates four Nile cruises offering three- to six-day itineraries. All the vessels are luxurious but there are differences between them. Shehrayar and Shehrazad have 31 spacious cabins (the largest currently on the Nile) with two bathrooms per cabin. Each cruise boat accommodates a maximum of 70 guests on any trip. They also have their own berths at Aswan and Luxor – no tramping through several other boats to get to the shore. Philae has large French windows in all its 58 cabins. It also has a small gym. All vessels offer excellent service, all meals are included, and there are fully guided tours. Cabins have air-conditioning, satellite TV, mini-bar and safe. Facilities include restaurant, bar, shop and pool. Major credit cards.

Recommended Restaurants

Egypt has a wide range of international restaurants, often linked to large hotels, where you can enjoy food prepared and served to a high standard. These are more expensive than local restaurants but no more than you would pay for an equivalent meal at home, and often a little less. All hotels welcome non-residents at their restaurants.

The following recommendations include Egyptian and international restaurants in all price ranges in the main tourist centres. Prices are indicated in Egyptian pounds, but you may occasionally find menus priced in US dollars and may even be charged in US dollars. Where reservations are recommended it is stated in the description. To make a reservation from within the town or city, do not dial the area code.

The following is a price guide for a meal for one, excluding alcohol:

$$$$$	over 250LE
$$$$	180–250LE
$$$	100–180LE
$$	50–100LE
$	under 50LE

ALEXANDRIA AND THE MEDITERRANEAN

Coffee Roastery $–$$ *48 Shari Fuad, tel: 03-4834363*. Western-style café-restaurant where young Alexandrian students and families come to hang out, chat, meet friends and watch the latest MTV movies on the large screen. Great for either coffee or lunch, with good coffee, milk shakes, fresh fruit juices, and a large selection of sandwiches and salads. No alcohol.

Samakmak $$$–$$$$ *42 Qasr Ras at-Tin, tel: 03-4811560*. The best fish and seafood restaurant in town, with excellent grilled fish and fabulously fresh seafood, including a wonderful crab *tagen* (stew) and big shrimps. Open daily 11am–11pm. Major credit cards.

Splash $$–$$$ *Hilton Alexandria Green Plaza, Smouha, tel: 03-4209120*. Located in a popular shopping mall, this relaxed Italian restaurant is a great place to people-watch as it would seem that all of Alexandria comes here for a stroll. Major credit cards.

Trianon $ *56 Midan Saad Zaghoul, Alexandria, no phone.* Tea, ice cream, pastries and light snacks are served in this authentic Art Deco tea room harking back to the days of European rule. A visit is thoroughly recommended, if only to take in the bustling Alexandrian atmosphere. Open daily 9am–11pm. Cash only.

ASWAN

Aswan Moon $–$$ *Corniche an-Nil, Aswan, tel: 02-2316108.* This floating restaurant on the Nile is a good and simple Egyptian eating place, with nothing fancy on the menu. The grilled chicken, kebabs and *kofta* are all good, though the pizzas may disappoint. The view at sunset is fabulous, and the atmosphere relaxed. Alcohol is served. Open daily 11am–11pm. Major credit cards.

Nubian House $$$ *On the Nile, 700m beyond the Nubian Museum, Aswan, tel: 097-2326226.* Delightful restaurant built on top of a cliff with stunning views over the Nile. Tea buffet served on the terrace at sunset. Both the architecture and the well-prepared food are authentically Nubian in style. Open daily 11am–11pm. Major credit cards.

The 1902 $$$$$ *The Old Cataract Hotel, Abtal at-Tahrir Street, Aswan, tel: 097-2316000.* The grand Moorish-style dining room frequented by Winston Churchill and Agatha Christie is one reason to eat at this restaurant – the atmosphere takes you back to the days of the Grand Tour, with muffled conversations and clinking glasses. A shame, though, that there isn't a terrace. The food is mainly southern European and Egyptian. Open daily noon–3pm, 7pm–midnight. Formal dining; reservations recommended. Major credit cards.

CAIRO

Abu al-Sid $$$–$$$$ *157 Shari' 26 Yulyu, Zamalik, tel: 02-7359640 or 7497326.* Trendy, atmospheric Egyptian restaurant with over-the-top Oriental décor, artworks by local painters and sweeping Egyptian music. The traditional Egyptian dishes are delicious and served with alcohol, and there's even a *sheesha* (water pipe) if you feel so inclined.

Alfi Bey $$ *3 al-Alfi Street, Downtown, tel: 02-5771888*. This restaurant serves very simple Egyptian food, specialising in *kofta*, kebabs and stuffed pigeon. A loyal local clientele and ancient waiters mean there is a genuine Egyptian atmosphere. Open daily 6pm–11pm. Cash only. No alcohol.

Andrea's $ *59–60 Marioutiya Canal, Giza, tel: 02-3831133*. Good Egyptian restaurant famous for its spit-roasted chicken served with tasty *mezze* and salads. In summer you can eat in the airy gardens, and there is a dining room for the chillier winter evenings. Lunchtime is often busy with tour groups, so for a more authentic atmosphere come in the evenings, although be sure to bring mosquito repellent. Open daily noon–midnight. Cash only.

L'Aubergine $$$$ *5 Shari' al-Sayed al-Bakri, Zamalik, tel: 02-7356761*. A popular gathering place for vegetarian expats and young Egyptians before they move on to noisier places. The upstairs bar is popular and has an in-house DJ.

La Bodega $$$$ *Balmoral Hotel, 157 Shari' 26 Yulyu, Zamalik, tel: 02-7356761*. Stylish bar, cocktail lounge and restaurant on the first floor of a period building with a sophisticated Asian interior, a beautiful crowd and wonderful fusion cooking. Open daily 7pm–1am. Major credit cards.

Felfela $–$$ *15 Hoda Shaarawi St, at Tahrir Square, tel: 02-3922833*. Located near the Egyptian Museum, Felfela is a Cairo institution patronised by Egyptians and tourists alike. The authentic Egyptian menu consists of many *hummus*, *falafel* and other vegetarian dishes, as well as kebabs, pigeon stuffed with bulgur, and marinated quail. The atmosphere is congenial, but service is slow and portions are small – however at these prices a number of tasty specialities can be sampled. Open daily, 11am–1am. Cash only.

Fish Market $$$$ *Americana Boat, 26 Giza Street, Giza, tel: 02-5709693.* Wonderful selection of the freshest fish and seafood, cooked to perfection and served with a delicious array of *mezze* and salads. The atmosphere and Nile views are particularly recommended at night. Open daily 12.30pm–2.30am. Major credit cards. Central Cairo branch at the Cairo Marriott Hotel, Zamalek, *tel: 02-3408888.*

Khan al-Khalili Restaurant $$$–$$$$$ *5 al-Baddistan Lane, Khan al-Khalili, Cairo, tel: 02-5903788.* Located in the heart of Islamic Cairo and the Bazaar, this is a safe but pricey haven catering to tourists and tour groups, and run by Oberoi Hotels. The décor and menu are Egyptian. The adjacent café is good for tea and light refreshments. Open daily 11am–11pm. Major credit cards.

The Moghul Room $$$$$ *Mena House Oberoi Hotel, Pyramids Road, Giza, tel: 02-3833222.* The best Indian cuisine in the city – which is perhaps not surprising, given the Oberoi's Indian antecedents – combined with plush décor, attentive service and an intimate ambience. Live Indian music. Open daily noon–3pm, 7.30pm–12.30am. Reservations are recommended. Major credit cards.

Sabaya $$$$$ *Semiramis Intercontinental, Corniche an-Nil, Garden City, tel: 02-7957171.* Superb Lebanese restaurant with a contemporary feel and exquisite Middle Eastern cuisine. In addition to the à la carte menu, Sabaya is famous for its homemade dishes prepared on request – visit in advance to check the menu. Great wine list and elegant service. Open daily for lunch and dinner.

Sequoia $$–$$$ *end of Abu al-Feda Street, Zamalek, tel: 02-7350014.* Great location on the tip of the Gazirah Island, overlooking the Nile on all sides, and a wonderful place for relaxing with friends, either on the terrace or in the tent-like structure. This is where hip Cairo mixes with middle-class families and expats. Just lie back on one of the comfortable sofas and have a drink or smoke a *sheesha* (with over 30 flavours of tobacco to choose from), or try out the excellent Oriental menu. Book ahead as this place is hugely popular. Open daily 2pm–1am. Major credit cards.

LUXOR

Al-Moudira Restaurant $$$$–$$$$$ *Daba'iyya, West Bank Luxor, tel: 012-3251307.* The most romantic hotel in Luxor serves the best food in town in its sumptuous Lebanese-Mediterranean restaurant. Most vegetables come from their own organic garden, and the setting is superb. Open daily noon–11pm. Reserve in advance. Major credit cards.

Jamboree $$–$$$ *Muntazah Street (near the Brooke Hospital for Sick Animals), Luxor, tel: 012-7813149.* This British-owned café/ restaurant is impeccably clean with stiff table linen and freshly cut flowers. You can find Egyptian specialities here, but most clients seem to prefer the English/Indian menu and the Italian dishes. Open daily 10.30am–2.30pm, 6.30pm–11pm. Cash only.

Oasis Cafe $–$$ *Sharia Dr Labib Habashi, East Bank, tel: 012-3367121.* This delightful café-restaurant in a 1920s building is in the centre of town. The café is cosy, decorated with local furniture and pretty watercolours, and there is good music in the background. The food is great, with sandwiches, grilled meat, salads, pastas and a recommended brunch. Excellent value.

Sofra $$ *90 Sharia Mohamed Farid, al-Manshiya quarter, tel: 095-2359752, <www.sofra.com.eg>.* An excellent Egyptian restaurant in a funky old villa in the centre of Luxor. A wide selection of salads, *mezze* and grilled main courses are served in several dining rooms or on a wonderful terrace. No alcohol, but lots of fresh juices. Very good value.

Tutankhamun $–$$ *South of the ferry landing dock on the West Bank, Luxor, tel: 095-2310118.* The cheerful and very friendly chef, Mahmoud, who trained at a five-star restaurant, serves up simple but delicious Egyptian dishes, particularly *tagens* (stews in clay pots), as well as his famed chicken with rosemary. Pleasant terrace overlooking the Nile. Open daily 10am–10pm. Cash only.

RED SEA AND SINAI

Hard Rock Café $–$$$ *Marina Street, Na'ama Bay, Sharm al-Shaykh, tel: 062-3602665.* Burgers, sandwiches and salads from the worldwide café chain – one of the town's most popular night spots with good music and friendly staff. Open daily 1pm–1am. Major credit cards.

Joker $$–$$$ *Sigala Square, Hurghadah, tel: 065-3512921.* Simple but very popular fish restaurant where you buy your fish and seafood by weight, decide how to have it cooked and then have it served with bread and fresh salads. No alcohol. Open daily noon–11pm. Major credit cards.

Liquid Lounge $$ *Sharia Sheraton, Sigala.* Very popular and hip beach bar, under the same management as the Papas Bar nearby. Serves good-value international lunch and dinner under the stars. Open daily 9am–3am. Major credit cards.

Nesima Restaurant $$–$$$ *Nesima Hotel, Mashraba, Dahab, tel: 062-3640320.* Delicious, charming and very relaxed beach restaurant with a mixed international and Egyptian menu, where fish is a main feature. Perfect for a laid-back lunch, but even better for a romantic candle-lit dinner right on the beach. Open daily 11am– midnight. Major credit cards.

La Rustichella $$$–$$$$ *Just at the back of Na'ama Bay, Sharm al-Shaykh, tel: 062-3601154.* This superb Italian restaurant is deservedly popular with the many Italians on holiday in Na'ama Bay. The pasta dishes are excellent, and the fish dishes are particularly well cooked.

INDEX

---

 pocket guide

Egypt

Eleventh Edition 2008
Reprinted 2008

Written by Lindsay Bennett
Updated by Sylvie Franquet
Managing Editor: Clare Peel
Series Editor: Tony Halliday

All Rights Reserved
© 2008 Berlitz Publishing/Apa Publications GmbH & Co. Verlag KG, Singapore Branch, Singapore

Printed in Singapore by Insight Print Services (Pte) Ltd, 38 Joo Koon Road, Singapore 628990. Tel: (65) 6865-1600. Fax: (65) 6861-6438

Berlitz Trademark Reg. U.S. Patent Office and other countries. Marca Registrada

Photography credits
All photography by Axel Krause except: Action Press/Rex Features 22; akg London 19; Apa 20; Pete Bennett 24, 34, 38, 46, 50, 55, 57, 60, 69, 74, 83, 95, 98, 101; Berlitz 27, 32, 44, 47, 48–9, 66, 75, 90, 100; Luc Chessex 16, 58, 59, 61, 63; Sarah Louise Ramsey 6, 11, 15, 29, 30, 33, 42, 67, 72, 84, 96, 105.
Cover picture: Jose Fuste Raga/Corbis

Every effort has been made to provide accurate information in this publication, but changes are inevitable. The publisher cannot be responsible for any resulting loss, inconvenience or injury.

Contact us

At Berlitz we strive to keep our guides as accurate and up to date as possible, but if you find anything that has changed, or if you have any suggestions on ways to improve this guide, then we would be delighted to hear from you.

Berlitz Publishing, PO Box 7910, London SE1 1WE, England.
fax: (44) 20 7403 0290
email: berlitz@apaguide.co.uk
www.berlitzpublishing.com